BUSINESS ECONOMICS IN A RAPIDLY-CHANGING WORLD

AF734417

BEHAVIORAL ACCOUNTING

BUSINESS ECONOMICS IN A RAPIDLY-CHANGING WORLD

Additional books in this series can be found on Nova's website under the Series tab.

Additional e-books in this series can be found on Nova's website under the e-book tab.

BUSINESS ECONOMICS IN A RAPIDLY-CHANGING WORLD

BEHAVIORAL ACCOUNTING

ANDREAS HELLMANN
EDITOR

New York

Copyright © 2013 by Nova Science Publishers, Inc.

All rights reserved. No part of this book may be reproduced, stored in a retrieval system or transmitted in any form or by any means: electronic, electrostatic, magnetic, tape, mechanical photocopying, recording or otherwise without the written permission of the Publisher.

For permission to use material from this book please contact us:
Telephone 631-231-7269; Fax 631-231-8175
Web Site: http://www.novapublishers.com

NOTICE TO THE READER

The Publisher has taken reasonable care in the preparation of this book, but makes no expressed or implied warranty of any kind and assumes no responsibility for any errors or omissions. No liability is assumed for incidental or consequential damages in connection with or arising out of information contained in this book. The Publisher shall not be liable for any special, consequential, or exemplary damages resulting, in whole or in part, from the readers' use of, or reliance upon, this material. Any parts of this book based on government reports are so indicated and copyright is claimed for those parts to the extent applicable to compilations of such works.

Independent verification should be sought for any data, advice or recommendations contained in this book. In addition, no responsibility is assumed by the publisher for any injury and/or damage to persons or property arising from any methods, products, instructions, ideas or otherwise contained in this publication.

This publication is designed to provide accurate and authoritative information with regard to the subject matter covered herein. It is sold with the clear understanding that the Publisher is not engaged in rendering legal or any other professional services. If legal or any other expert assistance is required, the services of a competent person should be sought. FROM A DECLARATION OF PARTICIPANTS JOINTLY ADOPTED BY A COMMITTEE OF THE AMERICAN BAR ASSOCIATION AND A COMMITTEE OF PUBLISHERS.

Additional color graphics may be available in the e-book version of this book.

Library of Congress Cataloging-in-Publication Data

Behavioral accounting / editor, Andreas Hellmann (Department of Accounting and Corporate Governance, Faculty of Business and Economics, Macquarie University, NSW, Australia).
pages cm
Includes index.
ISBN 978-1-62618-039-0 (soft cover)
1. Accounting--Psychological aspects. 2. Financial statements. I. Hellmann, Andreas editor of compilation.
HF5636.B44 2013
657.01'9--dc23

2013002530

Published by Nova Science Publishers, Inc. † New York

CONTENTS

Preface **vii**

Chapter 1 Information Behavior of Private Investors in the Age of the Internet **1**
Andreas Hellmann, Simone Domenico Scagnelli and Bernd Jörs

Chapter 2 Homo Economicus in Accounting and Finance: Lessons from Behavioral Economics **31**
Andreas Hellmann

Chapter 3 Enforcement and Managers' Financial Reporting Behavior: A Review of the Empirical Enforcement Literature **55**
Brigitte Eierle and Miriam Schleicher

Chapter 4 A Road towards Enhanced Corporate Governance: (Re)conceptualizing the Accounting Profession through an Integrated Educational Framework **85**
Nicholas McGuigan and Thomas Kern

Chapter 5 Neurosciences: The Next Frontier of Behavioral Accounting? **97**
Andreas Hellmann and Lurion De Mello

Index **103**

PREFACE

Accounting research is diverse; however, mainstream accounting research is often dogmatizing an image of efficient capital markets in which investors (and other stakeholders) make rational decisions by evaluating all available alternatives. In order to make such decisions, they interpret so-called neutral and unbiased information (which is equally available to all market participants) and select the alternative with the highest return or lowest risk. Behavioral accounting is challenging such simplistic assumptions. It is concerned with the explanation and prediction of human behavior in an accounting context such as the usefulness of financial statement data, materiality judgments, decision effects of alternative accounting procedures, and the impact of variables such as culture on the interpretation and application of accounting pronouncements. This book gives holistic and innovative insights into new developments in behavioral accounting, and provides evidence that behavioral aspects cannot be ignored in the interpretation and application of accounting information. Of particular importance in this volume is giving voice not only to aspects of behavioral research that have been most recently in the limelight, but also to contributions that are just beginning to make their mark such as neuroaccounting. Chapter 1 examines internet financial reporting. Specifically, it outlines how corporations utilize the internet for providing financial information and discusses the online behavior of private investors. Chapter 2 outlines the *homo economicus* model which is often implicitly used as theoretical underpinning in mainstream accounting research. It critically discusses the shortcomings of this model and calls for more interdisciplinary research in accounting focusing on behavioral aspects of preparers, users, and other stakeholders. Chapter 3 provides a framework for analyzing the impact of enforcement actions on management`s accounting behavior and reviews current empirical research in this area. Chapter 4 critically discusses integrated reporting and specifically how integrated reporting may influence the accounting profession and accounting education. Chapter 5 introduces a potential new stream of accounting research, which may be called “Neuroaccounting”. Specifically, this chapter argues that research can be enhanced if it moves away from crude approaches that classify people into groups to approaches that is based on hard scientific data.

In: Behavioral Accounting
Editor: Andreas Hellmann

ISBN: 978-1-62618-039-0
© 2013 Nova Science Publishers, Inc.

Chapter 1

INFORMATION BEHAVIOR OF PRIVATE INVESTORS IN THE AGE OF THE INTERNET

Andreas Hellmann[1*], Simone Domenico Scagnelli[2†] and Bernd Jörs[3‡]

[1] Department of Accounting and Corporate Governance
Macquarie University, Sydney, Australia
[2] Department of Management
University of Turin, Turin, Italy
[3] Department of Information Science and Engineering
Darmstadt University of Applied Sciences, Darmstadt, Germany

ABSTRACT

The internet is increasingly used by corporations for investor relation purposes and by investors as source of information. This chapter outlines how corporations incorporate this technology in their financial reporting strategies, and reviews relevant literature in regard to the online behavior of private investors. Specifically, the chapter outlines the development of the internet from its beginning in the 1960s to a major source of information for private investors, and highlights the different types of online information disseminated by corporations. It identifies that prior

* Tel: 61 2 9850 4055, Email: andreas.hellmann@mq.edu.au.
† Tel: 39 011 6706025, Email: simone.scagnelli@unito.it.
‡ Tel: 49 6151169398, Email: bernd.joers@h-da.de.

research focused on the internet financial reporting practices of companies, and largely ignored information needs of investors. This chapter suggests that future research about the effectiveness of internet financial reporting should incorporate a user-perspective in their research design. For this purpose, it introduces Wilson's model of information (seeking) behavior, which may be useful in guiding future research examining the information behavior of investors. Specifically, this model depicts information seeking behavior as an iterative process which is influenced by several factors such as the context of information needs and the socio-cultural environment. Prior research focused largely on a description of internet financial reporting based on content analysis. Such research can be enhanced using experimental and qualitative research approaches derived from Wilson's model. This would be useful because it clearly shows that information seeking behavior is mainly driven by behavioral aspects such as human relationships.

Keywords: Internet, financial reporting, information seeking, investment decisions

1. Introduction

Investors can be differentiated into two main groups, namely institutional investors such as fund managers, strategists, asset allocators, risk managers, corporate financiers and analysts, and those individuals who invest their private savings from time to time or on a regular basis. In order to make their investment decisions, both groups rely on information provided by companies. As a result, companies engage heavily in investor relation activities to communicate with potential and existing investors. The primary objective of investor relation activities is to provide information needed by investors in order to make capital allocation decisions (Deller, et al. 1999). For this purpose, financial statements are typically regarded as primary source of information because they provide detailed information on public corporations' economic activities and are directly available from companies or discussed in condensed form in the financial press (Palepu, et al. 2007, p. 12).

However, financial statements are complex products and both institutional and private investors may refer to them differently. Due to their professional background, institutional investors are likely to spend more time analyzing financial statements prior to making their investment decisions. However, private investors may not have the accounting knowledge to evaluate financial statements, and those who do not seek guidance from brokers or other intermediaries, are unlikely to consult financial statements. They may seek information which is easier to comprehend than financial statements. For this purpose, the Internet is increasingly used by corporations to attract investors scattered around the world and to disseminate not only financial statements but also press releases, speeches, investor conference calls, links to products such as broker reports, or other investor relations information such as policies on corporate governance or corporate social responsibility (Ashbaugh, et al. 1999, Ettredge, et al. 2001, Lymer & Debreceny 2003, Robbins & Stylianou 2003, Bollen, et al. 2006).

Internet financial reporting changed the way corporations and private investors interact with each other not only because new types of investor relations information is available to investors but also because such information is available in real time. Motivated by the increasing importance of the Internet for both corporations and investors, this chapter has the following objectives: (1) to explain the nature of corporate information which is presented on corporate web sites; (2) to provide a better understanding of the information seeking behavior of financial information users; and (3) to provide a general introduction to some key theoretical concepts utilized in information science research. Importantly, these theoretical concepts may be useful in future research examining information behavior of investors. For the purpose of this chapter, information behavior describes the ways human beings interact with information, namely information seeking and utilizing information (Case 2007, p. 5). The focus in on information seeking; issues in regard to utilizing information is discussed in chapter 2.

The rest of the chapter is structured as follows. First, relevant literature is examined with a focus on information content of corporate web pages. Next, private investors and their information seeking behavior are described. Next, some theoretical concepts from information sciences are discussed that may enable accounting researchers to improve the research methodology, theoretical development, and hypothesis formulation for future research into the behavior of financial information users. Finally, concluding comments are made.

2. Internet Financial Reporting

The Internet has provided corporations with a new channel to communicate with investors and other stakeholders around the world. Today, investor relations web sites provide financial and other information in real time, which investors are able to access independent of their physical location. Investors can also subscribe to a mailing list and have real time information delivered to their inbox. This section provides some background regarding the development and content of the investor relations web sites, which is important for a better understanding of information seeking behavior of investors. It is structured as follows. First, general information on internet financial reporting is provided. Second, benefits and issues related to internet financial reporting are discussed. Third, types of information provided on corporate web sites are described.

2.1. Development of Internet Financial Reporting

Originating from research conducted in the United States in the late 1960s, todays Internet is a global system of interconnected computer networks (Comer 2007, p. 62). Since its origin, the Internet has developed into the world largest computer network with over 2 billion users (Internet World Stats 2011). Many applications and services have been devised that use the Internet, such as Email and the World Wide Web ("The Web"). The Web is a particularly popular internet application linking together textual or non-textual information stored on many computers (Comer 2007, p. 208). This information is then gathered by individuals using powerful search engines from giant companies such Google and Microsoft. Since the mid-1990s, a large number of organizations are using the Web to create web sites in order to provide corporate information to Internet users. For example, using a sample of 290 nonfinancial U.S. firms, Ashbaugh et al. (1999) documented internet financial reporting practices of 177 firms and provide evidence that large firms (as defined by assets) in particular are integrating the Internet in their financial reporting strategies. Similarly, Debreceny and Gray (1999) show that 49 of the 50 largest industrial US corporations established corporate web sites by 1996. Debreceny and Gray (1999) also show that corporate web sites are not a phenomenon limited to the United States. In Europe, 44 of 45 large European corporations based in the UK, Germany and France also featured corporate web sites in 1999 and in Germany Deller et al. (1999) found that 76% of companies listed on the German Stock Index had a web site.

The corporate web sites surveyed by these early researchers included pieces of financial information not necessarily combined in a dedicated section on the corporate web site. This changed fundamentally in the past decade and today, internet financial reporting is an integral part of corporate web sites and financial reporting information is typically included in a dedicated investor relations section. For example, all 30 corporations included in the German Stock Index[1] maintain not only corporate web sites but also feature a specific investor relations section.

This clearly shows that corporate web sites including an investor relations component are important communication channels and that the Internet plays a vital role in modern trading markets. Indeed, in a recent guideline on the use of company web sites, the Securities and Exchange Commission (2008, p. 4) in the United States considers "company web sites as a significant vehicle for the dissemination to investors of important company information". The Securities and Exchange Commission (2008, p. 11) concludes that "the availability of information in electronic form is the superior method of providing company information to most investors, as compared to other methods".

The Securities and Exchange Commission was the first regulator to use the internet since 1995 to receive and disseminate corporate filings through its Electronic Data Gathering, Analysis and Retrieval system (also commonly known as EDGAR). Such systems also exist in countries like China, where listed companies are required since 2000 are required to provide their annual reports, interim reports, and prospectuses on the web sites of the China Securities Regulatory Commission, the Shanghai Stock Exchange, and the Shenzhen Stock Exchange. However, Xiao et al. (2004) point out that data submitted to systems of regulators only contain information that is required to meet the regulatory standards and does not include timely information on stock prices and other corporate news. These data depositories are not perfect substitutes for investor relations web sites (Xiao, et al. 2004). In certain trading markets, however, companies are required by regulators to establish and maintain corporate web sites. For example, the New York Stock Exchange requires most of its listed companies to establish and maintain their own web sites, which is highlighted in Section 303A.04 of the listed companies manual. It requires that companies "must make its nominating/corporate governance committee charter available on or through its website" (New York Stock Exchange 2012).

[1] The German Stock Index (Deutscher Aktienindex) is a stock market index consisting of the 30 major German companies trading on the Frankfurt Stock Exchange. In 2012, these companies are Adidas, Allianz, BASF, Bayer, Beiersdorf, BMW, Commerzbank, Daimler, Deutsche Bank, Deutsche Börse, Deutsche Post, Deutsche Telekom, E.ON, Fresenius Medical Care, Fresenius SE, Heidelberg Cement, Henkel, Infineon Technologies, K+S, Linde, Lufthansa, MAN, Merck, Metro, Munich RE, RWE, SAP, Siemens, Thyssen Krupp, Volkswagen.

2.2. Benefits and Issues Related to Internet Financial Reporting

There are several advantages for companies to establish corporate web sites and a dedicated investor relations section, most notably the notion that web sites enable companies to make “information available to investors quickly and in a cost-effective manner” (Securities and Exchange Commission 2008, p. 6). Similarly, Ashbaugh et al. (1999), Ettredge et al. (2001), and Lodhia et al. (2004) point out that, using corporate web sites, companies can provide a quantity and timeliness of information to private investors previously available only to institutional investors. They argue that corporate web sites enable companies to make available new kinds of information such as transcripts or audio versions of analyst conference calls, thereby reducing the costs of printing and mailing traditional financial information. Furthermore, companies are able to communicate directly with a broad range of stakeholders. The reason for this is that the demographics of internet users are more inclusive of varying educational and income levels compared to traditional communication methods (Perry & Bodkin 2000). The internet also allows one-way, two-way and multi-way communication which permits the development of highly interactive applications (Debreceny, et al. 2001). This may result in tailored information which can satisfy the diverse information needs of users. Specifically, interactive applications allow companies and users to create an unlimited number of independent perspectives over the same web site (Debreceny, et al. 2001).

However, internet financial reporting may also have some disadvantages relative to traditional financial reporting. For example, Debreceny et al. (2002) argue that the rapidly increasing amount of information provided on corporate web sites may cause a condition called information overload[2]. This condition highlights that too much presented information may cause confusion which may make it difficult for people to make appropriate decisions (Eppler & Mengis 2004). Importantly, many aspects of internet financial reporting are not regulated. This can make it difficult to control both the content of information and the context in which information is used, which may result in security and trust issues (Debreceny & Gray 2001, Lymer & Debreceny 2003,

[2] The problem of information overload may be reduced by the development of the eXtensible Business Reporting Language (XBRL) led by the American Institute of Certified Practicing Accountants. Using XBRL, documents can be created where specific pieces of information are tagged in plain language. This allows for easy exchange of information between formats and tailor-made extraction of data. Hodge et. al. (2004) find that users who use XBRL are better able to acquire and integrate information than those who do not use it.

Xiao, et al. 2002). The unregulated nature of internet financial reporting also impacts the audit of a corporation. Using a sample of the 50 largest industrial U.S. corporations, Debreceny and Gray (1999) found that 34 had annual reports on their web sites but only 19 of these included the auditor's report. Analyzing the web sites of 250 companies based in the USA, UK, Canada, Australia and Hong Kong, Allam and Lymer (2003) found audit reports on the web sites of 240 companies and suggest much greater availability of audit reports. However, they noticed that 111 companies provided unsigned reports. Similarly, Fisher et al. (2004) found that 79 per cent of 188 companies in New Zealand feature an auditor report without a scanned signature of the auditor, which makes it difficult for users to make an assessment concerning the authenticity of the audit report document. This is problematic for investors because financial information is considered reliable when independent auditors certify it. As financial reports are normally delivered on just one part of a corporate web site, misleading or unreliable information may potentially be presented alongside the financial data for which the auditor is primarily responsible (Gowthorpe 2004). Lymer and Debreceny (2003) point out that in such cases corporations would give investors the incorrect impression that all information on the web site has been audited.

Moreover, the internet makes financial reporting portable and globally accessible, which, in turn, makes it more difficult to regulate cross-border financial reporting. The reason for this is that the internet is decentralized and any government can only regulate actions taken in its own territory. This problem also applies to enforcing regulations, especially as there is no control over the context of the financial information. In other words, enforcement bodies have no control over other (non-audited) information on a web site, which may not even be presented under the heading 'investor relations'. Despite the increasing use of the internet, internet financial reporting is not comprehensively regulated. As highlighted above, regulators such as the Securities and Exchange Commission in the United States provide guidance on internet financial reporting, and stock exchanges such as the New York Stock Exchange require selected information to be made available on corporate web sites. However, the two globally accepted accounting regimes, namely U.S.-GAAP and International Financial Reporting Standards (IFRS), do not feature any standard regulating internet financial reporting. This means that, provided that it is not fraudulent, corporations are largely free to present the quantity and type of investor relations information that they desire on their web sites.

2.3. Information Provided on Corporate Web Sites

The previous section clearly shows that internet financial reporting is an essential strategy for corporations. Maintaining an investor relations web site and the extent of using the internet for financial reporting may depend on many factors such as firm size, leverage, industry, listing status, and profitability. Several studies provide evidence that firm size is the most significant factor affecting internet financial reporting and the amount and nature of information that is provided (Ashbaugh, et al. 1999, Craven & Marston 1999, Ettredge, et al. 2001, Hedlin 1999, Marston 2003, Marston & Polei 2004, Xiao, et al. 2004). For example, Debreceny et al. (2002) find that voluntary adoption of internet financial reporting in 22 countries is associated with company size and listing on an U.S. stock exchange. They also find that larger companies are more likely to provide financial information on the internet than smaller companies.

The extent to which corporations use the Internet changed considerably since the beginning of its widespread commercial adoption in the mid-1990s. Lymer and Debreceny (2003) highlight three stages for implementing internet financial reporting in a company's communication strategy: First, companies use the Internet only for distributing the existing printed annual report. In this stage, the internet is simply used as a new distribution channel. Second, they change the presentation format of the annual report and disclose the information in a form with which web browsers and search engines can readily interact. Third, they provide not only the annual report on web sites but also additional information that cannot be produced cost-effectively in a printed format such as corporate presentations and conference calls. Additionally, interactive tools may be provided which can be used to analyze the information directly on the web site.

At the early stage of internet financial reporting, Lymer et al. (1999) surveyed the 30 largest companies in 22 countries and found that internet reporting primarily duplicated the printed financial statements in an electronic format. In recent years however, two types of information are disseminated. One type consists of reports that have been filed with a regulator such as the Securities and Exchange Commission. These reports include mainly financial information. The second type is all other voluntary information, mostly including nonfinancial data (Ettredge, et al. 2002).

By analyzing the web sites of 402 U.S. companies, Ettredge et al. (2001) find that the most common accounting items on corporate web sites are quarterly reports and annual reports. They also find that the most common non-accounting items are financial news and links to stock data. Other common financial information on web sites include condensed financial statements, weekly, monthly and quarterly operating statistics, and pending or recently completed mergers and acquisitions. Other common nonfinancial information includes reports on labor relations and corporate social responsibility (Ashbaugh, et al. 1999). Table 1 summarizes common types of information found on corporate web sites.

Table 1. Information provided on corporate web sites

Financial disclosures	Nonfinancial disclosures
Analyst fact books	Business strategies
Back orders	Directors and officers
Earnings announcements	Environmental practices
Global operations	Environmental reports
Financial statements	Industry specific reserves
Labor contracts	Labor relations
Mergers and acquisitions	Philanthropic activities
Monthly/weekly sales	Press releases
Segment disclosures	Size of customer base
Stock plans	Social responsibilities
Stock price and performance	Year 2000 updates
Financial highlight summary	Chairman's message
Auditor's report (none, signed, not signed)	Corporate information
Balance sheet	Customer profile
Income statement	Employee profile
Cash flow statement	Social reports
Statement of shareholder's equity	Management report
Notes to financial statements	Vision statement
Segment report	Calendar
Statement of Directors	Speeches
Proxy Statements	Legal disclaimer
Financial Ratios (in context only, tables and in context)	Director's biographies
Consolidated Statement of operations	Email news alert
Quarterly Statement	Audio content
Analyst (lists of or links to analysts following the company)	Video content
Current stock price	Presentations
Dividend reinvestment plan information	
Historic share price	
Forecast information	

Source: Abdelsalam, et al. 2007, Ashbaugh, et al. 1999, Gowthorpe 2004, Lodhia et al. 2004, Lymer & Debreceny 2003, Marston & Polei 2004, Pirchegger & Wagenhofer 1999.

Ashbaugh et al. (1999) find substantial variation in the quality of companies' internet financial reporting practices. Specifically, they find that some firms provide more timely financial disclosures such as monthly sales, while other firms report outdated financial data such as two-year old annual reports. Ettredge et al. (2001) provide evidence that companies tailor content specifically for web sites. Specifically, 17% of companies from their sample of 402 U.S. companies provide excerpts from annual reports which usually include complete income statements (71.6%) and balance sheets (64.2%) but few cash flow statements (34.3%) and statements of shareholders' equity (26.9%). Notes were only found among 20.9% of the excerpts.

Additional to the increasing amount of information provided on web sites, its presentation is becoming more complex (Debreceny, et al. 2002). In regard to presentational features, Marston and Polei (2004) find that annual reports are typically disclosed in HTML and PDF versions, and that video files are becoming increasingly important for communication purposes. The use of graphical information in annual reports increased substantially in recent years (Beattie & Jones 1997). By using the emotive power of elements such as design, color and music in the context of the multi-dimensional possibilities of the internet, companies may have greater exponential power to influence decision makers than in the two-dimensional format of the traditional annual report. This allows companies to emphasize the positive and provide interpretation for potentially negative information.

3. Information Seeking Behavior of Private Investors

Private investors are increasingly being regarded as important contributors on capital markets (Vogelheim, et al. 2001). Important reasons for this development may be that, due to technology advancements such as the Internet, private investors can easily and quickly participate in, or withdraw from, the market, and can receive information for relatively low cost (Peress 2005, Ynesta 2008). Indeed, ownership in equities is an attractive investment choice for individuals around the world, which is reflected in studies aiming to identify the ownership structure of listed companies. In a comprehensive share ownership study across European countries, the Federation of European Securities Exchanges (2008) found that individual investors amount to 14% of the market value of listed shares in Europe[3]. Moreover, it reported that market participation of individuals varies across European countries. For example, Italy is reported as having a high rate of individuals' market participation at 26,6%, Germany is reported as having a moderate level of 13,3%, and the Slovak Republic with the smallest level of European countries at 2% (Federation of European Securities Exchanges 2008). Relative to these figures from European countries, the U.S. is having the highest level of individuals' market participation with a rate of 36,6% (Fox & Lorsch 2012). These figures show that equity ownership is regarded as a main source of wealth for individuals.

This section provides a better understanding of private investors with respect to their online information behavior. As highlighted above, an important dimension of the ways human beings interact with information is information seeking. While institutional investors can easily access specialized databases and often have direct contact with companies' investor relations staff, private investors often lack a similar direct and easy access. As a result, the availability of information on the internet would represent useful support for them. In 2008, the Securities and Exchange Commission examined what kind of information sources on the internet are used by investors for their investment decision. The Securities and Exchange Commission found that corporate web sites of individual companies are the most important information source (frequently used for information seeking by 38% of investors), followed by private financial investment information web sites (24%), the web sites of specific funds (10%), search engines such as Yahoo (9%), and news web sites (8%) (Securities and Exchange Commission 2008). Interestingly, female investors regard corporate web sites of individual companies as being more important for investment decisions than male investors. Specifically, the Securities and Exchange Commission (2008) found that 49% of female investors refer to the web sites of individual companies for information seeking purposes, compared to 42% of male investors.

The literature on information available on the internet described in the previous section is largely descriptive and consists mainly of surveys of current reporting practices (for example Ashbaugh, et al. 1999, Ettredge, et al. 2001). While these studies provide important insights into the development of internet reporting, they do not consider the information needs of private investors. In other words, the studies highlighted in the previous section are

[3] This report has been published in the context of the Global Financial Crisis, which negatively impacted global financial markets and caused loss of financial wealth.

not providing evidence about the usefulness of information provided on web sites for private investors. Despite the growing use of the internet for disseminating financial information, there is little evidence to suggest that internet-based information has become increasingly useful for users. Only limited research is investigating what kind of information provided on the internet is considered by investors as being important and useful. This is surprising because Gowthorpe (2004) revealed that corporate managers tend to use their experience (or visit the web sites of competitors to get new ideas about information content) to assume investor's needs in an unsystematic way in order to design their web sites.

There are only few studies that have examined the effectiveness of web sites as perceived by investors. Beattie and Pratt (2003), for example, examined user groups, namely expert users, private shareholders, finance directors, and audit partners in regard to their attitudes toward different kinds of electronically provided information, their perceptions about the usefulness of different navigation and search aids, and their views on the portability of information under different formats. They found that most user groups rely on key management information, favor a free search function integrated on a web site, and prefer layered and pre-packaged information, periodic updating, and indexing. Hodge and Pronk (2006) found that private investors rely more on management's discussion of financial results than on financial statements. They also found that investment familiarity (i.e., whether investors are evaluating a current investment or researching a new investment) affects the type of financial information they view within a financial report. Specifically, they found that investors evaluating a current investment conducted their own investigation of the main financial statements more often than investors researching a new investment. Debreceny et al. (2001) examined desired information content attributes of accounting professionals and academics and found that traditional elements of the financial statements (including the main financial statements, notes, and the auditors' report) are the most highly ranked information attributes. They also found that information such as performance forecasts, the vision statement, and background information such as customer and employee profiles, were not rated as highly as traditional content attributes. Debreceny et al. (2001) argue that poor web site design and site functionality may cause disorientation and cognitive overload, and found that the form of information presented on web sites had an impact on the behavior of the participants. Specifically, they found that download time is a concern for participants which may negatively impact their willingness to open large documents[4]. However, a study by Mezick (2001) involving 97 U.S. investors, found that the majority of investors saw the internet as a reliable source of financial information compared to other sources.

Mainstream accounting and finance research has been built on the notion that human beings make rational investment decisions by evaluating all risks and returns of all possible investment options to arrive at an investment portfolio with the highest return or lowest risk (Hellmann & Scagnelli 2011). However, it is important to note that the increased amount of information available online, new kinds of electronically provided information, and the design and functionality of web sites and content may affect decision making of private investors. For example, the availability of information through the internet can cause an illusion of knowledge and control[5] (Barber & Odean 2001). If private investors place online orders directly without human intermediaries or personal advisors, they tend to be overconfident in regard to their knowledge, exhibit a confirmation bias and hindsight bias[6] (Daniel, et al. 2002, Kourtidis, et al. 2010). Research provided evidence suggesting that the confidence of investors in their forecast accuracy tends to be higher than the actual accuracy if more information is presented (Hoge 1970, Oskamp 1965, Peterson & Pitz 1988, Slovic & Corrigan 1973). As a result of increased information, accurate predictions may decline and heuristics are likely to be used during the investment decision process[7] (Keller & Staelin 1987, Stewart, et al. 1992, Nofsinger 2005.). A recent study involving 1500 Portuguese private investors provides evidence that the internet is also affecting trading frequency of investors (Abreu & Mendes 2012). Specifically, they find that overconfident investors trade less frequently when they collect information via friends and family and not from the internet, compared to non-overconfident investors who trade more frequently when they use specialized sources of information such as corporate websites (Abreu & Mendes 2012)

In summary, very few studies have attempted to describe the use of web sites by investors and there is little empirical research on user preferences for information provided on the internet. A possible reason for this gap in the

---

4 It has to be noted that download speed increased for many internet users since the time of Debreceny et al.'s (2001) study. Because of the rapid changes in internet technologies, their results may also quickly change.

5 Illusion of control can be defined as believe that personal involvement can influence the outcome of chance events (Presson & Benassi 1996).

6 See chapter 2 for further discussion on biases.

7 Heuristics in this context are defined as the use of experience and practical efforts to answer questions or to improve performance (Fromlet 2001).

literature might be that web-based financial reporting is a relatively new phenomenon. However, such research is urgently needed given the increasing importance of the internet for private investors. The next section provides an overview of information seeking theories which may help guiding future research in this area.

4. Information Seeking Theories

4.1. Historical Roots

Information behavior research started at the beginning of the 20th century and is described by Bates (2010, p. 2381) as "the many ways in which human beings interact with information, in particular, the ways in which people seek and utilize information". As a result of improvements in information retrieval methods and tools, information behavior studies focused the research interests on behavior scientific questions. The scientific roots of information behavior research lie in the traditional library and information sciences (LIS). As early as in 1948, the Royal Society Scientific Information Conference in London focused with selected topics on information seeking behavior. Wilson (2000, p. 50) considers this conference as the starting point for extensive research activities on modern information seeking behavior. One focus was on information retrieval (IR), which is a combination of quantitative and qualitative methods in the information sciences to examine the information needs of users. Specifically, IR aims to match the information needs of users with documents or other sources on the basis of structured or less structured questions adopting technology and algorithms. The efficiency of those automated algebraic and probabilistic information retrieval techniques and matching processes are typically summarized in performance and correctness indictors such as "precision", "recall" or "fall-out". Web search engines, for example, work on the basis of such algorithmic-based information retrieval models and principles (Kuropka 2004).

However, in the early days of information science research there was a large gap between the precision and recall of the founded documents and the information needs of the users. A pure technological view of information retrieval methods was not sufficient enough for a substantially and satisfying explanation of users' information needs and information behavior. In order to improve retrieval-, search- or information systems and to reduce information seeking and processing times, it was necessary to extend existing research by focusing on human-oriented and user-centered research questions. Bates (2010, p. 2381) describes the driving forces of the beginning of research activities on these behavior-oriented questions as follows:

> "Librarians wanted to understand library users better, government agencies wanted to understand how scientists and engineers used technical information in order to promote more rapid uptake of new research results, and social scientists generally were interested in the social uses of information in a variety of senses…Within library and information science, these various streams of research are drawn on for what they can contribute to a richer understanding of information behavior."

As a result, information behavior research shifted from a system-oriented approach to a user-orientated approach. The first comprehensive collection of research studies on information science were published by Davis and Bailey in the 1960s in their "*Bibliography of use studies*". In this collection, Davis and Bailey (1964) defined their research on human information behavior as "use studies". Two years later, Menzel (1966) introduced the term "information seeking" in his publication "*Information needs and uses in science and technology*". This was the beginning of concrete research interests on user interaction with information within LIS and it was the breakthrough of a new research field "information seeking". It is interesting to note that "information seeking" remained the specialist term for all behavioral studies in LIS for a relative long time. Since the early 1990s, when behavioral approaches became more and more relevant and commonly used in different science disciplines, the term "information seeking" was subsumed under the term "information behavior".

Several conferences in the 1970s continued to focus on information needs of users and information behavior, especially in the area of "information seeking behavior" or "information search behavior". The 1970s were also the time in which the area of computer science enriched research on data and information in several disciplines including the humanities. Investigations into requirements relevant to satisfy users' needs were concerned almost entirely with how a user navigated a given system and what he or she could do with the data made available by the information systems (Wilson 2000, p. 49). However, research in that area was not concerned about what kind of information is needed.

Tom Daniel Wilson was among the first to study information needs in LIS in the 1980s who became later one of the most influential researchers in that specific research field in LIS. Wilson was one of the first researchers who developed various models of information behavior till the end of the 1990s (for example, Wilson 1981, 1997, 1998, 1999, Wilson, et al. 2002, Wilson & Walsh 1996). Wilson (2005, pp. 33-34) claims that his framework is not derived from any theory proposed by other writers but from an analysis of human information behavior, partly a priori, but also from the detailed analysis of the information behavior of social workers and their managers carried out as part of Project INISS[8].

Wilson's research accelerated interest in and lay ground for more information behavior research in LIS. For example, the compendium "Theories of Information Behavior" edited by Fisher et al. (2005) includes the great number of 72 conceptual frameworks about this phenomenon. This publication provides a state of the art overview in information behavior research. Theoretical frameworks about human information seeking processes, information management, the (interactive) sharing of information and the use patterns of information are in the center of this compendium[9]. It presents theoretical frameworks and modeling activities in information behavior of scientists from different international schools, which are, however, primarily initiated by Wilson's fundamental theoretical work. Another example is "A philosophy of Informing Science" published by Cohen in 1999. Driven by Wilson's work on information behavior, Cohen introduces the notion of informing science which focuses on users and that they are provided with information, in a form, format, and schedule that maximizes its effectiveness"(Cohen 2009, p. 6). Cohen later founded the multidisciplinary "Informing Science Institute" (ISI, Santa Rosa, USA) in 1999 with representatives of different scientific disciplines including computer science, biology, linguistics and information science. The major focus of informing science therefore is concentrated on the following research fields:

1) Biological and psychological issues in how clients attend, perceive, and act on information provided,
2) The decision-making environment itself, including its sociology and politics,

---

[8] INISS: information needs in local authority social services departments

[9] Topics, for example, include cognitive work analysis, information poverty, Dervin's sense-making theory, diffusion theory and information behavior, ecological theory of human information behavior, everyday life information seeking, flow theory, the imposed query, information encountering, information horizons, nonlinear information seeking, the principle of least effort, the ELIS model, Nan Lin's theory of social capital, information use environments, web information behaviors and world wide web information seeking.

3) Issues involving the media for communicating information,
4) Error, bias, misinformation, and disinformation in informing systems (Cohen 2009, p. 6).

Cohen's theoretical framework supports a multidisciplinary approach and he argues that because both the informer and the client are influenced by human-relationship issues, they are best examined by those fields of study that deal with understanding cognitive, behavioral and social issues. Further, he concludes that information needs of an individual are complex and are a function of context, environment, social or job role or task, and the individual's psychology (Cohen 2009, p. 8). This is a broader understanding of information behavior and incorporates findings from behavioral sciences and neurobiology.

The third example for the relevance and influence of Wilson's work on information behavior research is the organization of the annual "Information Behavior Conference", organized by Information Seeking in Context (ISIC). The first conference was held in 1996 in Tampere, Finland, which focused on all research areas concerning information seeking, information searching, use and sharing in specific contexts, in virtual social networks, in real and virtual communities, during decision-making processes on the basis of different theories (social network theory, actor network theory, cultural-historical activity theory, genre theory, communication theory), the determinants of information requirements (for information systems) and information needs, the design of information delivery systems, the management of collaborative information seeking and searching processes, the information architecture and the communication of information[10].

In summary, multidisciplinary research approaches and a combination of approaches from natural sciences and humanities on information behavior dominate research efforts today. Adopting theoretical developments from the early researchers outlined above, information behavior research has been conducted in various professional contexts including health sciences, law and business (Bates 2010, p. 2384). The next section provides more insights into Wilson's model of information (seeking) behavior and other theories that influenced the development of that model.

---

[10] http://informationr.net/isic/

4.2. General Information Behavior Theories

It is important to note that there is no single information behavior theory. However, Wilson's model of information (seeking) behavior can be regarded as a major framework in information behavior. In general, information behavior theories aim to find answers, for example, to the following questions:

- What are the relevant determinants of human information behavior within the process of information seeking, information searching and information use resulting from a special information need?
- Which sources and information channels are important and why?
- What are the reasons for active, motivated, self-determined human information behavior, for example within a face-to-face communication, or more inactive (passive) information behavior with a reception of information without a concrete intention to handle (i.e. watching TV advertising)?

4.2.1. Wilson's Model of Information (Seeking) Behavior

Wilson considers a precise conceptual delimitation of the different research disciplines within the information behavior of greatest importance. He defines the term "information behavior" as follows:

> Information Behavior is the totality of human behavior in relation to sources and channels of information, including both active and passive information seeking, and information use. Thus, it includes face-to-face communication with others, as well as the passive reception of information as in, for example, watching TV advertisement, without any intention to act on the information given (Wilson 2000, p. 49).

In a general model of information behavior, Wilson (1999) tried to integrate his research findings of longtime research studies (which started in 1981) and theoretical consideration on information behavior in a general theoretical model of information (seeking) behavior focused on problem-solving (Wilson 2000, p. 53). This model is depicted in Figure 1.

Wilson (2000) tried to find explanations on how information seeker or users try to identify and satisfy their information needs. One of the most relevant research questions for Wilson was: Which variables determine mostly information seeking behavior? He described his theory approach as a "cycle of information activities" where the information needs are only secondary needs, following and caused by other primary needs, which can have affective, cognitive or/and physiological origins (impetus). These information needs activate a more or less intentional information behavior to collect new or confirming information. Activating determinants may include curiosity (non-utilitarian, common), meaning seeking, order seeking, or an understanding of an unknown phenomenon.

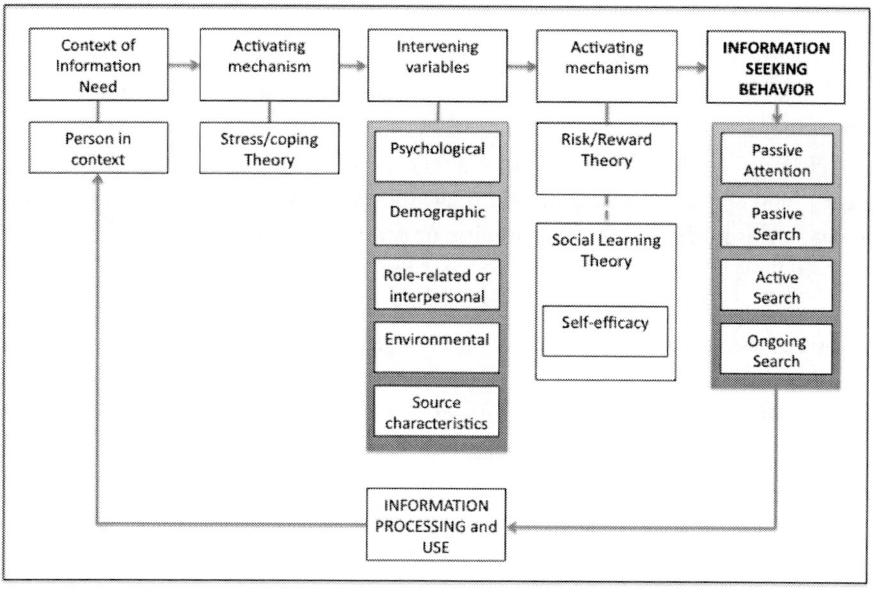

Source: Wilson, T. D. (2000). Human Information Behavior. *Informing Science*, 3(2), p. 53.

Figure 1. Wilson's model of information (seeking) behavior.

Importantly, the context of information needs, such as the social and work role, the work environment, the social cultural environment, the political-economic and the physical environment, has to be considered as it has great influence on the information behavior of every person as information seeker. Attention should be paid to several intervening variables such as psychological, demographical, role-related or interpersonal, and environmental variables and source characteristics. They induce new activating mechanism within the cycle of information activities, which can be explained by the risk and reward theory or the social learning theory (self-efficacy). After these steps the information process starts: the purposive information seeking activity. Wilson (2000, p. 49) describes information seeking behavior as the purposive seeking for information as a consequence of a need to satisfy some goal. In the course of seeking, the individual may interact with manual information systems (such as a newspaper or a library), or with computer-based systems (such as the World Wide Web). Importantly, the information need and its context determinate the information seeking behavior. It also determines the relevance of sources and the use intensity of the different sources.

4.2.2. Ellis's Behavioral Model of Information Seeking Strategies

Wilson (2000) integrated Ellis's behavioral model of information seeking strategies (Ellis 1987, Ellis, et al. 1993) in his information seeking behavior model. Ellis analyzed the iterative seeking behavior process and its different stages, and the main question included the following: What characterizes the typical information seeking behavior or strategy of information seeker? Ellis (1987, 1993) suggested iterative process includes the following steps:

- First step (Starting): An information seeker is aiming to get an overview by asking other people or by using a first source. Here, the initial search for information begins. The information search often starts with more or less familiar sources, especially sources which are known to the information seeker.
- Second step (Browsing or chaining or monitoring): Ellis describes "browsing" as semi-directed or semi-structured searching in certain sources (Wilson 2000, p. 52). Important for browsing are tables of contents, lists, (web) links, names, persons, organizations, and so on. Choo et al. (1998) explain that browsing takes place in many situations in which related information is grouped together according to subject affinity. "Backward chaining" occurs when the information seeker follows footnotes and citations in known material or "forward chaining" from known items through citation indexes (Wilson 2000, p. 52). "Chaining" indicators include, for example, topical documents, citation frequency, and actuality of the document, the author, cost and time exposure. "Monitoring" means that the information seeker keeps up-to-date (Wilson 2000, p. 52).
- Third step (Differentiating): This is the first stage where an evaluation takes place. It has an important filtering purpose, which strongly depends on the experiences of the information seeker with the sources or on reviews or personal recommendations of other people. The information seeker attempts to judge the quality, usefulness and

relevance of the search outcomes. Here the information seeker is filtering the amount of information obtained (Wilson 2000, p. 52).

- Fourth step (Extracting): The information seeker is able to select and identify the relevance of his information sources and material, mostly by concentrating on the most relevant core sources.
- Fifth step (Verifying): Is the obtained information correct and reliable? The information seeker is "checking the accuracy" (Wilson 2000, p. 52) of his information outcomes.
- Sixth step (Ending): The whole seeking process ends and the information seeker combines the information outcome(s) with his personal knowledge.

Ellis information seeking model outlined above was modified by other researchers. Meho & Tibbo (2003), for example, complemented Ellis' behavioral model of information seeking strategies by adding tree additional steps, namely "Accessing" (to full text documents), "Networking" (direct and indirect communication with other people about the information results) and "Information Managing" (information storage).

Already in 1998, Choo et al. (1998) tried to verify Ellis' information seeking process theory on the internet. On the empirical basis of questionnaires, personal interviews with managers and IT specialists, and on the basis of using customer-developed tracker applications for the monitoring of the participants' web browser activities, they studied the different web information seeking patterns. Choo et al. (1998) viewed the web as a hyperlinked information system distributed over numerous networks, where most of the information seeking behavior categories in Ellis' model was already being supported by capabilities available in common web browser software. Similar to Ellis's theory, Choo et al (1998) suggest the following steps:

- First step (starting): The information seeker can start from familiar or new websites by identifying the pages with include information of interest.
- Second step (chaining): Here the information seeker follows (hypertextual) links to other websites with substantial content both forward and backward.
- Third step (browsing): The focus of this information seeking step is the scanning of (top-level) selected web sites.

- Fourth step (differentiating): Parallel to or after the third step the information seeker can bookmark relevant sources for revisiting and references.
- Fifth step (monitoring): The user can receive site updates or can prepare summaries of interest or make reports.
- Sixth step (extracting): Now the information seekers is satisfied with his/her information and can extract the necessary content of a local web site or he/she is disappointed and starts from the beginning again.

Choo et al. (1998) pointed out that findings appeared to support the behavioral model, both in terms of the modes of scanning and the moves of web information seeking associated with each mode. Overall, the study suggests that a behavioral framework that relates motivations (the strategies and reasons for viewing and searching) and moves (the tactics used to find and use information) may be helpful in analyzing web-based information seeking.

4.2.3. Kuhlthau's Stage Model

Kuhlthau (1991, 1993) emphasizes the importance of the emotional experience for information seeking behavior. The first step of her information seeking model, the initiation, is accompanied by a certain degree of uncertainty. This means that thoughts are regarded as general and vague, ambiguity dominates, and the first activity is to recognize the information need. The second step should lead to optimistic feelings, when the so-called "selection" gives the chance to select and to identify the relevant topics and information sources. The third step, the exploration, can lead to some confusion, frustration or doubt. The task of the information seeker is to investigate relevant information. The fourth step, the formulation, should give the information seeker more clarity. He or she can define more precisely the concrete topics. As a result, the satisfaction increases. With the fifth step, the collection, Kuhlthau wanted to express that the information seeker earns more self-confidence by gathering the relevant information, his or her interest increases and he or she knows more about the meaning of the obtained information. The information seeking process ends with the sixth step, the presentation, where the satisfaction can reach its highest point or the disappointment of an unsuccessful or failed search dominates.

Wilson proposed to integrate Ellis' "Behavioral model of information seeking strategies" and Kulthaus' "Stage model" with his general information behavior model (Wilson 2000, p. 55). Wilson emphasizes that the consequences of such a target-oriented, intentional information seeking behavior, is characterized by passive attention, active or passive search or ongoing search. For those search activities, Wilson (2000, p. 49) defines an own behavior segment:

> The Information Searching Behavior is the 'micro-level' of behavior employed by the searcher in interacting with information systems of all kinds. It consists of all the interactions with the system, whether at the level of human computer interaction (for example, use of the mouse and clicks on links) or at the intellectual level (for example, adopting a Boolean search strategy or determining the criteria for deciding which of two books selected from adjacent places on a library shelf is most useful), which will also involve mental acts, such as judging the relevance of data or information retrieved.

The last step of the iterative information cycle process included in Wilson's model of information (seeking) behavior is information processing and use. It is one of the crucial points in Wilson's theory and he speaks of "Information Use Behavior" as the third partial form of human information behavior. Wilson (2000, p. 50) defines it as follows:

Information Use Behavior consists of the physical and mental acts involved in incorporating the information found into the person's existing knowledge base. It may involve, therefore, physical acts such as marking sections in a text to note their importance or significance, as well as mental acts that involve, for example, comparison of new information with existing knowledge. Depending on the degree of information satisfaction, the information seeker stops the process or starts again with the definition of his concrete information need(s).

CONCLUSION

The rapidly changing business environment in today's globalized world is forcing corporations to provide timely and relevant information to decision makers. Given that 2 billion people routinely access the internet (Internet World Stats 2011), maintaining a web site to disseminate financial information has become an important strategy that corporations adopt to provide relevant information to decision makers. Many corporations not only disclose an electronic copy of the annual report on their web sites, but maintain investor relations sections on their corporate web sites. These investor relations sections typically feature a range of different types of information, ranging from text-based information such as reports on labor relations and corporate social responsibility to interactive and multimedia tools such as video files and customized search algorithms. Indeed, internet financial reporting may enable companies to make customized information available to investors quickly and in a cost-effective way. It can help corporations to provide a quantity and timeliness of information to private investors which were previously available only to institutional investors. This is especially important because in many capital markets, private investors are increasingly regarded as being important capital contributors (Vogelheim, et al. 2001).

Despite the trend that financial information is increasingly disclosed on corporate web sites, very little is known about the information behavior of private investors. Specifically, prior literature largely focused on the supply-side (i.e. what types of information are provided on corporate web sites) and did not rigorously examine how users access and use online financial information. In other words, it effectiveness of current internet financial reporting practices remains unclear. This is an important issue because it has been argued that information overload may cause confusion and make it difficult for users to make appropriate decisions (Eppler & Mengis 2004). As such, this chapter argues that future research needs to incorporate both the information provided by corporations and also the information needs of private investors. Importantly, the medium internet can influence the information behavior of investors and aspects such as presentation of information, design, and usability should also be addressed in future research.

To guide future research in this area, this chapter outlines Wilson's model of information (seeking) behavior, which is a comprehensive framework from the library and information sciences. Specifically, this model outlines a cycle of information activities, and shows variables that determine information seeking behavior. It is a very general model that might help to explain the more fundamental aspects of human behavior by highlighting the importance of personal and environmental contexts. Importantly, information seeking behavior as described in this model is observable, whereas needs being internal mental states, are not. Wilson's model stresses the interrelated nature of theory in this field by incorporating Elli's behavioral characteristics of information seeking and Kulthau's treatment of the information search process, which have been also described in this chapter.

This chapter provides valuable insights into the context in which internet financial reporting is used and suggests that future research about the effectiveness of internet financial reporting is needed. For this purpose, researchers need to adopt a user-perspective in their research design. This would be especially useful for companies aiming to enhance their investor relations activities

REFERENCES

Abdelsalam, O.H., Bryant, S.M., Street, D.L. (2007). An examination of the comprehensiveness of corporate internet reporting provided by London-based companies. *Journal of International Accounting Research*, 6(2), 1-33.

Abreu, M., Mendes, V. (2012). Information, overconfidence and trading: Do the sources of information matter? *Journal of Economic Psychology*, 33(4), 868-881.

Allam,A., Lymer, A. (2003). Developments in internet financial reporting: Review and analysis across five developed countries. *International Journal of Digital Accounting Research*, 3(6), 165-200.

Ashbaugh, H., Johnstone, K.M., Warfield, T.D. (1999). Corporate reporting on the internet. *Accounting Horizons*, 13(3), 241-257.

Barber, B.M., Odean, T. (2001). The internet and the investor. *Journal of Economic Perspectives*, 15(1), 41-54.

Bates, M.J. (2010) Information Behavior, in *Encyclopedia of Library and Information Sciences, 3rd Edition*, M.J. Bates, M.N. Maack, eds., CRC Press, New York.

Beattie, V., Pratt, K. (2003). Issues concerning web-based business reporting: An analysis of the views of interested parties. *British Accounting Review*, 35(2), 155-187.

Beattie, V.A., Jones, M.J. (1997). A comparative study of the use of financial graphs in the corporate annual reports of major U.S. and U.K. companies. *Journal of International Financial Management and Accounting*, 8(1), 33-68.

Bollen, L., Hassink, H., Bozic, G. (2006). Measuring and explaining the quality of internet investor relations activities: a multinational empirical analysis. *International Journal of Accounting Informaiton Systems*, 7(4), 273-298.

Case, D.O. (2007). *Looking for information: A survey of research on information seeking, needs and behavior* (2 ed.). Elsevier, New York.

Choo, C.W., Detlor, B., Turnball, D. 1998. A Behavioural Model of Information Seeking on the Web. Preliminary Results of a Study of How

Managers and IT Specialists Use the Web, *ASIS Annual Meeting*. Pittsburgh.

Cohen, E.B. (2009). A Philosophy of Informing Science. *Informing Science*, 12, 1-15.

Comer, D.E. (2007). *The Internet Book* (4 ed.). Pearson Education, Upper Saddle River, New Jersey.

Craven, B.M., Marston, C.L. (1999). Financial reporting on the internet by leading UK companies. *European Accounting Review*, 8(2), 321-333.

Daniel, K., Hirshleifer, D., Teoh, S.H. (2002). Investor psychology in capital markets: evidence and policy implications. *Journal of Monetary Economics*, 49(1), 139-209.

Davis, R.A., Bailey, C.A. (1964). *Bibliography of Use Studies*. Drexel Institute of Technology, Philadelphia.

Debreceny, R., Gray, G.L. (1999). Financial reporting on the Internet and the external audit. *European Accounting Review*, 8(2), 335-350.

Debreceny, R., Gray, G.L. (2001). The production and use of semantically rich accounting reports on the internet: XML and XBRL. *International Journal of Accounting Information Systems*, 2(1), 47-74.

Debreceny, R., Gray, G.L., Mock, T.J. (2001). Financial reporting web sites: what users want in terms of form and content. *International Journal of Digital Accounting Research*, 1(1), 1-23.

Debreceny, R., Gray, G.L., Rahman, A. (2002). The determinants of internet financial reporting. *Journal of Accounting and Public Policy*, 21(4-5), 371-394.

Deller, D., Stubenrath, M., Weber, C. (1999). A survey on the use of the internet for investor relations in the USA, the UK and Germany. *European Accounting Review*, 8(2), 351-364.

Ellis, D. (1987). *The derivation of a behavioural model for information retrieval system design. Ph. D. Thesis*. Department of Information Studies, University of Sheffield, Sheffield.

Ellis, D., Cox, D., Hall, K. (1993). A comparison of the information seeking patterns of researchers in the physical and social sciences. *Journal of Documentation*, 49(4), 356-369.

Eppler, M.J., Mengis, J. (2004). The concept of information overload: A review of literature from Organization Science, Accounting, Marketing, MIS, and related disciplines. *Information Society*, 20(5), 325-344.

Ettredge, M., Richardson, V.J., Scholz, S. (2001). The presentation of financial information at corporate web sites. *International Journal of Accounting Information Systems*, 2(3), 149-168.

Ettredge, M., Richardson, V.J., Scholz, S. (2002). Dissemination of information for investors at corporate web sites. *Journal of Accounting and Public Policy*, 21(4-5), 357-369.

Federation of European Securities Exchanges (2008). Share ownership structure in Europe. Retrieved 11.11, 2012, from http://www.fese.be/_lib/files/Share_Owner ship_Survey_2007_Final.pdf

Fisher, K.E., Erdelez, S., Mc Kechnie, L. (2005). *Theories of Information Behavior. American Society for Information Science and Technology*. American Society for Information Science and Technology, Medford.

Fisher, R., Oyelere, P., Laswad, F. (2004). Corporate reporting on the Internet: Audit issues and content analysis of practices. *Managerial Auditing Journal*, 19(3), 412-439.

Fox, J., Lorsch, J.W. (2012). What good are shareholders?. *Harvard Business Review*, July-August, 49-57.

Fromlet, H. (2001). Behavioural finance-theory and practical application. *Business Economics*, 36(3), 63-69.

Gowthorpe, C. (2004). Asymmetrical dialogue? Corporate financial reporting via the Internet. *Corporate Communications: An International Journal*, 9(4), 283-293.

Hedlin, P. (1999). The internet as a vehicle for investor relations: The Swedish case. *European Accounting Review*, 8(2), 373-381.

Hellmann, A., Scagnelli, S.D. (2011). Behavioral Accounting: Shifting Away from Techniques to People, in *Advances in Business and Management. Volume 3*, William D. Nelson, ed., Nova Science Publishers, New York.

Hodge, F.D., Kennedy, J.J., Maines, L.A. (2004). Does search-facilitating technology improve the transparency of financial reporting? *Accounting Review*, 79(3), 687-703.

Hodge, F., Pronk, M. (2006). The impact of expertise and invstment familiarity on investors' use of online financial report information. *Journal of Accounting, Auditing and Finance*, 21(3), 267-292.

Hoge, R.D. (1970). Confidence in decision as an index of perceived accuracy of information processing. *Psychonomic Science*, 18, 351-353.

Internet World Stats. Internet world stats, Vol. 2012, Miniwatts Marketing Group, Bogota, 2011.

Keller, K.L., Staelin, R. (1987). Effects of quality and quantity of information on decision effectiveness. *Journal of Consumer Research*, 14(2), 200-213.

Kourtidis, D., Sevic, Z., Chatzoglou, P. (2010). Investors' trading activity: a behavioural perspective. *International Journal of Trade and Global Markets*, 3(1), 52-67.

Kuhlthau, C.C. (1991). Inside the search process: Information Seeking from the User's Perspective. *Journal of the American Society for Information Science and Technology*, 42(5), 361-371.

Kuhlthau, C.C. (1993). *Seeking meaning: A Process Approach to Library and Information Services*. Libraries Unlimited, Norwood.

Kuropka, D. (2004). Modelle zur Repräsentation natürlichsprachlicher Dokumente. Ontologie-basiertes Information-Filtering und -Retrieval mit relationalen Datenbanken. *Advances in Information Systems and Management Science*, 10, 1-264.

Lodhia, S.K., Allam, A., Lymer, A. (2004). Corporate reporting on the internet in Australia: An exploratory study. *Australian Accounting Review*, 14(3), 64-71.

Lymer, A. (1999). The Internet and the future of corporate reporting in Europe. *European Accounting Review*, 8(2), 289-301.

Lymer, A., Debreceny, R. (2003). The auditor and corporate reporting on the internet: Challenges and institutional responses. *International Journal of Auditing*, 7(1), 103-120.

Marston, C. (2003). Financial reporting on the internet by leading Japanese companies. *Corporate Communications: An International Journal*, 8(1), 23-34.

Marston, C., Polei, A. (2004). Corporate reporting on the internet by German companies. *International Journal of Accounting Information Systems*, 5(3), 285-311.

Meho, L.I., Tibbo, H.R. (2003). Modeling the information-seeking behavior of social scientists: Ellis's study revisited. *Journal of the American Society for Information Science and Technology*, 54(6), 570-587.

Menzel, H. (1966). Information needs and uses in science and technology. *Annual Review of Information Science and Technology*, 1, 41-69.

Mezick, E.M. (2001). Investing wisely: Individual investors as information seekers. *Journal of Business and Finance Librarianship*, 7(1), 3-23.

New York Stock Exchange. 2012. Listed Company Manual.

Nofsinger, J.R. (2005). *The Psychology of Investing*. Pearson Prentice-Hall, Upper Saddle River.

Oskamp, S. (1965). Overconfidence in case-study judgments. *Journal of Consulting Psychology*, 29(3), 261-265.

Palepu, K.G., Healy, P.M., Bernard, V.L., Peek, E. (2007). *Business analysis and valuation: IFRS edition*. Thomson, London.

Peress, J. (2005). *The Journal of Financial and Quantitative Analysis*, 40(3), 563-594.

Perry, M., Bodkin, C. (2000). Content analysis of Fortune 100 company web sites. *Corporate Communications: An International Journal*, 5(2), 87-96.

Peterson, D.K., Pitz, G.F. (1988). Confidence, Uncertainty, and the Use of Information. *Journal of Experimental Psychology: Learning, Memory, and Cognition*, 14(1), 85-92.

Pirchegger, B., Wagenhofer, A. (1999). Financial information on the internet: A survey of the homepages of Austrian companies. *European Accounting Review*, 8(2), 383-395.

Presson, P.K., Benassi, V.A. (1996). Illusion of control: A meta-analytic review. *Journal of Social Behavior and Personality*, 11(3), 493-510.

Robbins, S.S., Stylianou, A.C. (2003). Global corporate web sites: an empirical investigation of content and design. *Information and Management*, 40(3), 205-212.

Securities and Exchange Commission. 2008. Commission guidance on the use of company web sites. Washington.

Slovic, P., Corrigan, B. (1973). *Behavioral problems of adhering to a decision policy*. Institute for Quantitative Research in Finance, Napa.

Stewart, T.R., Heideman, K.F, Moninger, W.R., Reagan-Cirincione, P. (1992). Effects of improved information on the components of skill in weather forecasting. *Organizational Behavior and Human Decision Processes*, 53(2), 107-134.

Vogelheim, P., Schoebachler, D.D., Gordon, G.L., Gordon, C.C. (2001). The importance of courting the individual investor. *Business Horizons*, 44(1), 69-76.

Wilson, T.D. (1981). On user studies and information needs. *Journal of Documentation*, 37(1), 3-15.

Wilson, T.D. (1997). Information behaviour: An interdisciplinary perspective. *Information Processing and Management*, 33(4), 551-572.

Wilson, T.D. (1998). Exploring models of information behaviour: The 'Uncertainty' Project, in *Exploring the contexts of information behaviour, August 12-15*, T.D. Wilson, D.K. Allen, eds., Proceedings of the 2nd international conference on information seeking in context, Sheffield.

Wilson, T.D. (1999). Models in information behaviour research. *Journal of Documentation*, 55(3), 249-270.

Wilson, T.D. (2000). Human Information Behavior. *Informing Science*, 3(2), 49-55.

Wilson, T.D. (2005). Evolution in Information Behavior Modeling: Wilson's Model, in *Theories of Information Behavior. American Society for Information Science and Technology*, K.E. Fisher, S. Erdelez, L.

McKechnie, eds., American Society for Information Science and Technology, Medford.

Wilson, T.D., Ford, N.J., Ellis, D., Foster, A.E. (2002). Information seeking and mediated searching. Part 2: Uncertainty and its correlates. *Journal of the American Society for Information Science and Technology*, 53, 704-715.

Wilson, T.D., Walsh, C. 1996. Information behaviour: An interdisciplinary perspective, British Library Research and Innovation Report No. 10.

Xiao, J.Z., Jones, M.J., Lymer, A. (2002). Immediate trends in internet reporting. *European Accounting Review*, 11(2), 245-275.

Xiao, J.Z., Yang, H., Chow, C.W. (2004). The determinants and characteristics of voluntary internet-based disclosures by listed Chinese companies. *Journal of Accounting and Public Policy*, 23(3), 191-225.

Ynesta, I. (2008). *Households' Wealth Composition Across OECD Countries and Financial Risks Borne by Households*. OECD, Paris.

In: Behavioral Accounting
Editor: Andreas Hellmann

ISBN: 978-1-62618-039-0
© 2013 Nova Science Publishers, Inc.

Chapter 2

HOMO ECONOMICUS IN ACCOUNTING AND FINANCE: LESSONS FROM BEHAVIORAL ECONOMICS

Andreas Hellmann*

Department of Accounting and Corporate Governance, Faculty of Business and Economics, Macquarie University, Sydney, Australia

ABSTRACT

Mainstream accounting and finance literature is upholding an image of humans who make rational decisions by evaluating risks and returns of all available alternatives. It traditionally transformed humans into economic subjects who will rationally weight advantage against disadvantage and rigidly pursue their own interests. These characteristics of human decision making are incorporated in the concept of *homo economicus*, which significantly impacted the way accounting and finance theory has been developed. The objective of this chapter is to critically discuss the concept of the *homo economicus* and its application in accounting and finance research, based on findings from behavioral economics. Specifically, it shows that (1) humans rely on heuristics and biases for decision making, and (2) that the information which participants on financial markets are supposed to interpret for their decision making is not neutral, unbiased and value-free. The chapter

---

* Tel: +61 2 9850 4055; Email: andreas.hellmann@mq.edu.au.

argues that both accounting and finance research could be enhanced by methods and findings from behavioral economics.

Keywords: Behavioral Finance, Behavioral Accounting, Behavioral Economics, Homo Economicus, Economic Man, International Financial Reporting Standards

1. INTRODUCTION

In light of the current global financial crisis, it is difficult to imagine that economies in general and capital markets in particular are following rational economic strategies. Yet, it is often assumed in accounting and finance research that capital markets are efficient and that all participants would make decisions, namely selecting the alternative with the highest return or the lowest risk, based on a comparison of all available alternatives. Moreover, it is often assumed that investors would interpret unbiased information in order to make economic decisions. These simplistic assumptions are challenged by behavioral research in the areas of accounting and finance.

The emergence of the term *homo economicus* in the 19th century signified a conceptual centerpiece of economic theory that is still extensively used to simplify the many assumptions integrated within macro-economic models (Schneider 2010). Developed in order to depict the idea that people are rational if they engage in activities that will maximize their personal wellbeing, the purpose of the *homo economicus* as a symbolic metaphor is to enable economic phenomena to be explained and predicted with relative ease. Among the many different portrayals of economic agents, the term *homo economicus* is usually reserved for those who are rational in an instrumental sense. In its ideal case, *homo economicus* has complete and clear preferences, perfect information, and all the necessary brain power to analyze them. After deliberation, *homo economicus* selects the action that satisfies their preferences better than any other. The source or worth of these preferences is not questioned.

Since several decades, behavioral economics is integrating theory from psychology into economics to improve the explanatory power of economic models. Findings suggest that homo *economicus* does not always behave as predicted and people, for example, cannot process unlimited information, and use mental frames and heuristics to simplify complex decisions (see for example Kahneman and Tversky 2000, Gilovich, Griffin and Kahneman 2002,

Shafir 2004, De Bond 2005). Despite clear evidence that the concept of *homo economicus* has shortcomings, mainstream accounting and finance literature is largely applying quantitative models based on the concept of *homo economicus*. However, research in behavioral accounting and finance challenges the concept of *homo economicus* and denotes the study of accounting and finance based on assumptions about how people behave.

The purpose of this chapter is to show that the concept of *homo economicus* based on the rational behavior of users is too simplistic to be incorporated unrestrictedly in accounting and finance research. Importantly, research concerning investors and financial information is often entitled "Behavioral Finance", which focuses on the demand-side of financial information, namely on how investors make their decisions. This chapter argues that such a narrow view would ignore the supply-side, namely accounting information, which is a key source for financial decisions. It outlines that there is a strong relationship between behavioral finance and behavioral accounting, and that behavioral aspects on all dimensions of accounting are influencing the decision making of investors and other users of financial information. Specifically, it rejects the simplistic assumption that the information which investors and other stakeholders are supposed to interpret in order to make economic decisions is neutral, unbiased and value-free, and as such behavioral insights about how accountants prepare such information are needed.

This chapter may encourage researchers to move away from narrow approaches such as the *homo economicus* and develop new frameworks in accounting and finance, which focus on people and their behavior. It is structured as follows. First, it describes the concept of *homo economicus* and the development of behavioral economics. Second, major criticisms of *homo economicus* made by researchers in behavioral economics and psychology are outlined. Third, the relationship between behavioral accounting and behavioral finance is explained. Finally, concluding comments are made.

2. Behavioral Economics: The Mutual Basis for Behavioral Research in Accounting and Finance

Economics is the social science which analyzes the production, distribution, and consumption of goods and services. In other words, it is concerned with anything having to do with making a choice on allocating scarce resources. It is usually broken down into macroeconomics, which focuses on the aggregate economy, and microeconomics, which focuses on individuals. Early economists such as Leon Walras (1834-1910) and Paul Samuelson (1915-2009) greatly influenced the development of economic theory by using mathematics and statistics in order to explain the world. Wilkinson (2008, p. 10) argues that two main reasons motivated the strong influence of mathematics and statistics on economics: First, psychology as an academic discipline was at its infancy at this time; and second, many economists believed that the also-new science of economics would have a surer and more rigorous grounding, similar to that of the natural sciences, if it would be supported by mathematics. This influence was later accelerated by technological advancements, because with computers it became possible to build complex mathematical models of both markets and the economy as a whole (Wilkinson 2008).

In macroeconomics, the models developed were aimed to explain complex and large groups of individuals such as national economies. A model makes a series of simplifying assumptions from which it deduces how people will behave. For the purpose of explaining macro-economic relationships and to increase the predictive power of such models, the concept of *homo economicus*[1] was created. Indeed, the emergence of the term *homo economicus* in the 19th century signified a conceptual centerpiece of economic theory that is extensively being used to simplify the many assumptions integrated within macro-economic models. This model features two key characteristics in regard to human behavior: selfishness and rationality. It has to be noted that rationality can be defined and interpreted in many ways. In the context of the *homo economicus*, it is normally applied to decision-making and actions. Neoclassical theory equates rationality with the norm of expected utility maximization (Wilkinson 2008). Specifically, it features a rational disposition whereby the pursuit of self-interest is the underlying motivation towards the attainment of clearly defined preferences. Furthermore, *homo economicus* is presumed to possess perfect information where he has all available information (and also computing power to process them) to execute decisions that promote his egocentricity. Decisions are thus computed through rationally evaluating advantages and disadvantages to arrive at the economically optimal decision (Häring & Storbeck 2009, p. 2). Cultural dynamics and societal values are ignored in the computation of the best decision, as only economic considerations have a monetary value attached. In other words, *homo*

---

[1] Another term often used for *homo economicus* is the term "economic man".

economicus does not experience the sorts of sentiments that motivate people to return lost wallets to their owners with the cash intact or to contribute voluntarily to charities. On the contrary, personal material costs and benefits are the only thing *homo economicus* cares about. Consequently, ethics and other humanistic constituents such as empathy, trust, and justice are disregarded when arriving at the economically optimal decision.

The assumptions underlying the *homo economicus* model have been incorporated into many aspects of accounting and finance research. In the accounting field, White and Hanson (2000) point out that *Homo economicus* is a relatively unifying figure in the study of corporate annual reports. Indeed, characteristics of *homo economicus* have been incorporated into many theories adopted to study accounting, for example, shareholder theory, agency theory and legitimacy theory[2]. For example, agency theory focuses on the relationship between managers and investors. This relationship is characterized by contractual obligations and utility maximization. In this context Merkl-Davies and Brennan (2011, p. 416) point out that "both managers and shareholders are regarded rational, self-interested decision makers". They conclude that both corporate reporting and investment decisions follow strictly cost-benefit calculations based on mathematical models, which may justify impression management. In the finance field, mainstream finance literature has traditionally treated motives governing decisions as a non-issue and is largely applying quantitative models based on the concept of *homo economicus*. The classical assumption of *homo economicus* incorporated in traditional finance models is that the presence of a large quantity of buyers and sellers restricts the influence of individuals on the price of assets. This means that extreme and irrational decisions made by individuals would disappear in the mass of all decisions. In other words, financial markets have been describes as being efficient including market participants who share the characteristics of *homo economicus*.

However, with experimental economics[3], economic theories that relied on *homo economicus* were tested and anomalies such as irrational behavior and the importance of fairness discovered. Behavioral economics emerged as a

[2] It is beyond the scope of this chapter to provide a comprehensive review of this influence. The focus of this chapter is on behavioral insights from psychology that may be used to enhance accounting and finance research. See for example Rausch (2011) and White and Hanson (2000).

[3] Experimental economics is the application of experimental methods to study economic questions. As such, it is not a distinct area of study and rather a method of study that can be applied to any subject area.

result of these discoveries and is concerned with improving the explanatory power of economic theories by giving them a sounder psychological basis (Camerer & Loewenstein 2004, p. 3). By integrating social, cognitive, and emotional factors in understanding economic decisions, behavioral economics attempts to understand, for example, why humans are not always behaving like *homo economicus*. Findings from behavioral economics undermining the described key characteristics of this concept will be explained later in this chapter. Several refinements of this model have been proposed and some are outlined in the appendix of this chapter. The section below outlines how *homo economicus* influenced accounting and finance theory.

3. From Homo Economicus to Homo Sapiens

The main characteristics underlying *homo economicus*, namely selfishness and rationality, have been questioned in the past (Thaler 2000). Recall that *homo economicus* is also capable of understanding vastly complex puzzles and conducting endless optimizations. Behavioral economics verified that individuals are not purely self-absorbed in nature and more sociable than presumed by the concept of *homo economicus*. This is, for example, depicted through acts of altruism and reciprocation (Camerer & Fehr 2006). Furthermore, their decision making process is influenced by heuristics and biases, which affect their capabilities to conduct endless optimizations. This section outlines selected findings from behavioral economics and psychology that clearly show that people may not behave as the *homo economicus* model would predict.

3.1. Fairness and Reciprocation

Recall that economic agents are purely motivated by self-interest. However, there are many situations in life in which people's motivation is not purely driven by self-interest, for example when they are giving money to charities, completing tax returns honestly, engaging in voluntary unpaid work, or punishing free riders even when there is a cost in doing so. Such behavior could be described as either altruistic or spiteful. Wilkinson (2008, p. 328) defines altruistic behavior as "behavior which confers a benefit to others, while involving a cost to the originator of the behavior, with no corresponding material benefit", and spiteful behavior as "behavior that imposes a cost on others, while also involving a cost to the originator of the behavior, with no corresponding material benefit".

Both types of behavior involve benefits which are largely psychological in nature. Importantly, studies adopting game experiments[4] confirmed that such psychological incentives are driving people's motivation in situations outlined above. Common games used for this purpose include ultimatum bargaining games, dictator games, and trust games. Basic ultimatum games, for example, involve two players, namely a proposer and a responder. The proposer has to determine how to distribute a given amount of money. This means that the proposer can determine any amount of the given sum, which he demands for himself. For example, the proposer can offer anything between \$0 - \$100 if \$100 were to be distributed. Knowing this proposal, the responder can either reject or accept this proposal. In case the responder accepts, the proposer gets the proposed amount. In case the responder rejects, both players get zero (Güth et al. 1982). If both player act as *homo economicus*, it would be expected that the proposer offers the lowest amount aiming to keep the largest share for himself. For example, if \$100 is to be distributed, *homo economicus* is likely to propose only \$1 and keeping \$99 for him. *Homo economicus* as responder is likely to accept such an offer because \$1 is better than zero. However, evidence suggests that hardly anyone would accept such an offer. There might be several reasons for such a reaction. For example, Camerer and Fehr (2006) point out that there is a general tendency to engage in altruistic punishment when social norms have been disregarded. Furthermore, altruistic behavior may be influenced by ethical or religious beliefs. Studies indicate that most offers are between 0.4 and 0.5 of the surplus and that there are almost no offers below 0.2. Furthermore, low offers are frequently rejected (see for example, Camerer 1995, Hoffman, et al. 1996, List & Cherry 2000). Such results indicate that people do not behave as the *homo economicus* model would predict. Instead, responders are punishing proposals they regard as unfair, even at a cost to themselves. Related games are called dictator games. In such games, the responder's ability to reject an offer is removed. However, even in these scenarios, evidence suggests that proposers are making more generous offers than *homo economicus* would be expected to make (Hoffman et al. 1996, Heinrich et al. 2001).

4 The related research area is called Game Theory. Games in this context refer to an experimental design in which interdependency in decision-making exists.

Trust games have been initially designed by Berg et al. (1995) to study trust and reciprocity in an investment setting. Berg et al. (1995, p. 123) outline trust games as follows:

> Subjects in room A decide how much of their $10 show-up fee to send to an anonymous counterpart in room B. Subjects were informed that each dollar sent would triple by the time it reaches room B. Subjects in room B then decide how much of the tripled money to keep and how much to send back to their respective counterparts.

A prediction based on the *homo economicus* model would be that there will be no trust, because subjects in room B will never return anything. As a consequence, subjects in room A would not send anything. However, their findings suggest that subjects in room A were willing to place a trust in the belief that there would be reciprocity. Indeed, they found that subjects in room A sent money 55 out of 60 times. Similar to findings from ultimatum and dictator games, this is also an extensive anomaly in the *homo economicus* model.

3.2 Bounded Rationality

The experimental games outlined above provide clear evidence that not all humans are motivated purely by self-interest. The second main characteristic of the *homo economicus* model is rational behavior, which is normally applied in this context to decision-making and actions. The beginnings of a theory of bounded rationality were created by Simon (1957) who described decision making as a search process guided by aspiration levels. An aspiration level is defined in this context as "a value of a goal variable that must be reached or surpassed by a satisfactory decision alternative" (Selten 2001, p. 13). The search process continues until a satisfactory alternative is found which reaches or surpluses the aspirational levels on the goal variables. Importantly, Simon (1957) points out that the aspirational levels are not fixed and can be adjusted to the situation, namely they can be raised or lowered depending on how easy it is to find alternatives.

In the context of *homo economicus*, full rationality requires unlimited cognitive capabilities. However, the heuristics and biases outlined later in this section will clearly show that the cognitive abilities of humans are quite limited. Because of this reason, bounded rationality suggests that humans are guided by aspiration adaptation instead of utility maximization. In other words, humans are seeking a satisfactory solution rather than the optimal one.

In short, the term *bounded* in bounded rationality can refer to constraints in the mind. Kahneman (2003) explains that the cognitive architecture of the human mind comprises two systems, namely a system which operates automatically and is instinctively delivering an immediate response, and a system which requires concentration and deliberate effort to arrive at the answers to complex problems and fosters critical thinking. Among others, critical thinking is affected by two components, namely the attention span and memory capacity. In regard to decision making, issues arise from the fact that both attention span and memory capacity are limited in nature. As a result of this, humans simplify the available choice and may not act as the *homo economicus* model would predict. Specifically, bounded rationality postulates three constraints that obstruct optimization, namely limitations of the human mind, limitations of time, and limitations of information. Indeed, there is overwhelming experimental evidence for substantial deviations from rationality. Limitations of the human mind and limitations of time are discussed in this section; limitations of information are discussed in the next section.

Due to limited cognitive capacities, people need to rely on quick shortcuts, or heuristics, when they reason about unknown or uncertain aspects. Heuristics of reasoning are commonly used to explain biases, which are systematic deviations that are found between responses of respondents taking part in an experiment and normative solutions. Heuristics rely largely on past experiences and context information, and can be processed by the brain with relative ease. Gigerenzer and Goldstein (1996) and Gigerenzer et al (2002) suggest that judgment is based on a single cue. Specifically, they suggest that people search through cues in memory until they find a cue that enables a judgment[5]. Other common heuristics are the representativeness heuristic, availability heuristic, adjustment heuristic, and anchoring.

When people use the *representativeness heuristic* they are making a judgment of similarity. This means that people evaluate the probability that a subject belongs to a certain category based on the degree to which the subject resembles a typical item in the category (Kahneman & Tversky 1972, 1973, Tversky & Kahneman 1983, Kahneman & Frederick 2002). For example,

[5] It is important to note that such fast and frugal heuristics not necessarily result in inferior outcomes, and perform well when compared to more complex strategies that integrate available information (see Todd & Gigerenzer 2000, and Rieskamp, Hertwig and Todd, 2006, for a detailed discussion).

suppose Mark is a skinny, pale-skinned man with long hair, who wears glasses, and a T-shirt with a design related to comic books or science fiction, and we want to estimate the likelihood that he is a computer geek rather than an accountant. Most people may be eager to respond that Marc is much more likely to be a computer geek, because the described characteristics are thought to be representative traits for computer geeks but rather unusual ones for accountants. Tversky and Kahneman (1983) point out in this context that although the representativeness heuristic can lead to error, it may often lead to judgments that are sufficient if not perfect. The reason for this is that representativeness is related to frequency. Tversky and Kahneman (1983, p. 296) state that "common instances and frequent events are generally more representative than unusual instances and rare events". However, such responses are often biased because the probability of belonging to a certain category is influenced by many other important factors besides representativeness. Judgments based on representativeness can be problematic if events occur by coincidence and people fail to appreciate the nature of randomness. For example, the phenomenon known as *gambler's fallacy* describes that people treat the sequential outcomes of gambling devices as non-independent and behave as though the devices have a memory. Lottery players may not select numbers that appeared in a recent draw despite the fact that these numbers are just as likely to occur again as any other number. In the finance area, evidence suggests that the representativeness heuristic has implications to investment decisions. Specifically, investors may misinterpret recent achievements to be representative of what they can expect in the future (Benartzi 2001).

The *availability heuristic* describes that people judge probability or frequency based on ease of recall of relevant instances (Tversky & Kahnemann 1973). Specifically, Tversky and Kahneman proposed that events that were encountered recently are likely to have a greater impact on judgments. Also, familiar events or events for which it is easy to construct a vivid mental image may result in misinterpretations. The ease of recall of relevant instances and memory are influenced by the mood of a person. For example, Bower (1981) provides evidence that sad readers of a story attended more to sad materials, identified with a sad character from a story, and recalled more about that character.

The *anchoring-and-adjustment heuristic* describes that people make an estimate by using some starting value and then adjusting it to arrive at a final conclusion. Importantly, people typically fail to make sufficient adjustments away from the initial figure that they treat as an anchor (Tversky & Kahneman

1974). This occurs not only if anchors are relevant to the task. Tversky and Kahneman (1974) that people fail to make sufficient adjustments even if the anchor is irrelevant to the task. They provide evidence for this from a classic experiment for which they spun a number wheel and then asked participants to estimate whether the percentage of African countries that belong to the United Nations is higher or lower than the number on the wheel. Although the number on the wheel was a random number, subjects who received a high anchor made higher judgments on average than participants who received a low anchor (Tversky & Kahneman 1974). Such effects have been observed in a variety of domains including pricing (Mussweiler et al. 2000), negotiation (Galinsky & Mussweiler 2001), legal judgment (Chapman & Bornstein 1996, Englich & Mussweiler 2001), and accounting (Brown 1981). Bonner (2008, p. 168) argues that the *anchoring-and-adjustment heuristic* is especially relevant in the accounting and finance area because much of judgments and decision making is numerical in nature. For example, target prices of shares may be used as anchors by financial analysts independent of how reasonable these target prices are. Importantly, the literature provides evidence that this heuristic is powerful in influencing judgments. For example, participants have been found to use anchors even when explicitly warned not to do so (Wilson et al. 1996). Related to the *anchoring-and-adjustment heuristic* is the *hindsight bias*, which describes the tendency for people to be wise after the event. In other words, *hindsight bias* is used to "describe the observation that an uncertain outcome often seems more likely after it is known that the outcome has occurred" (Hardman 2009, p. 36).

Besides the heuristics outlined above, there exist other factors which bias people's judgments. For example, humans are generally overconfident and believe, among others, that they can predict the future better than they actually can, have better abilities than others, are being excessively optimistic about their future, able to control the outcomes of completely random events, and overestimate the reliability of their knowledge (for example, Lichtenstein et al. 1982, Cooper 1988, De Bondt 1998, Odean 1999, Barber & Odean 2002). Similarly, it is suggested that people regard new information asymmetrically after a decision has been made. This confirmation bias describes that information that is supporting the own hypothesis is often overvalued, and contradictory information is ignored or taken as exception (Koriat et al. 1980).

In summary, the cognitive abilities of humans are limited. For this reason alone, human's decision-making behavior cannot conform to the ideal of full rationality. However, the cognitive bounds of rationality are not the only ones. Imagine that you are a smoker and you may think that stop smoking is the only rational choice. Nevertheless, you decide not to take this option. In this scenario, your conclusion reached by rational deliberations is overridden by strong emotional impulses. This implies that the lack of complete control over behavior is not only due to cognitive bounds of behavior but also due to motivational ones.

This section highlighted that people do not have the computing power to analyze unlimited alternatives until the optimal solution has been found. It also outlined that heuristics are applied for judgments, and that these heuristics may result in biases. The discussion so far did not take into consideration that the information itself is not perfect. This is especially problematic in the finance area as most decisions are based on highly technical and so-called neutral information. The next section discusses issues resulting from accounting information which is clearly not objective, neutral, and value-free.

4. The Relationship between Behavioral Finance and Behavioral Accounting

Behavioral finance is highly related to behavioral economics and aims at improving the understanding of financial markets and participants. Mainstream finance literature has traditionally treated motives governing decisions as a non-issue and is largely applying quantitative models based on the concept of *homo economicus*. The classical assumption of *homo economicus* incorporated in traditional finance models is that the presence of a large quantity of buyers and sellers restricts the influence of individuals on the price of assets. This means that extreme and irrational decisions made by individuals would disappear in the mass of all decisions. Behavioral finance denotes the study of finance based on assumptions about how people behave. Confirmed by psychological experiments, behavioral finance established several limitations of the construct of *homo economicus* and shows that the trading decisions of individual investors are often psychologically biased. For example, Aspara and Tikkanen (2008) and Massa and Simonov (2006) show that individual investors are subject to emotional elements such as attitudes and brand familiarity despite having evaluated the financial position of a company. Various collected readings such as De Bond (2005), Gilovich, Griffin and Kahneman (2002), Kahneman and Tversky (2000), and Shafir (2004) incorporate psychological insight into decision making. As outlined above, this literature provides evidence, for example, that (1) people cannot process unlimited information and rather use mental frames to simplify complex decisions and heuristics to characterize and simplify data used in decision making, (2) time inconsistency exists in regard to choice, (3) biases such as optimism, conservatism, overconfidence and overreaction affect investors' decision making, and (4) asymmetric attitudes exist in regard to gains and losses.

Indeed, financial markets are not truly efficient and investors are humans with all their emotions and weaknesses. The examples above clearly show that investors and other capital market participants behave not as the *homo economicus* model would predict. However, there is another dimension that has not received sufficient attention. The information, which investors and capital markets participants are using in order to make their decisions, are largely based on accounting information. Similar to the finance literature, mainstream accounting literature tends to ignore behavioral aspects in the interpretation and application of accounting standards. This phenomenon is supported by assumptions made by accounting standards setters such as the International Accounting Standards Board (IASB). The IASB develops a set of globally accepted accounting standards. Indeed, it is highly successful to establish International Financial Reporting Standards (IFRS) as globally accepted accounting standards with over 115 countries permitting or requiring them to be used for financial reporting purpose[6]. The development of IFRS has been supported by the assertion that the application of IFRS is an important means of enhancing comparability of financial statements. An implicit assumption of the IASB seems to be that IFRS are objective, neutral, and value-free, because it assumes that financial statements are comparable across countries if accountants all over the world would apply IFRS. However, empirical evidence shows that accounting information cannot be value-free mainly because if the influence of contextual factors such as culture, which may affect professional judgments made by accountants (Hellmann, Perera et al. 2010). The judgment and decision-making literature provides clear evidence that accounting standards are applied inconsistently across countries for the reason that they are not objective, neutral, and value-free (for example, Doupnik and Richter 2003, 2004; Doupnik and Tsakumis 2004).

If accounting information is a requirement for making financial decisions, behavioral insights about how accountants prepare such information are needed. This would be particularly important for behavioral finance research,

[6] Because of their dominance in today's globalized world, IFRS and the IASB are used in this chapter as examples to highlight behavioral issues in financial accounting.

because participants on financial markets are largely influenced by so-called neutral and objective accounting information. The preparation and disclosure of accounting information is mainly determined by accounting standards such as IFRS, which need to be prepared by a standard setter and interpreted and applied by accountants. As such, behavioral issues in accounting can arise on the following three dimensions: (1) standard setting, (2) preparation of financial information, and (3) auditing. Firstly, accounting standard setting is a political process and the members of the IASB may be biased in regard to their opinion about specific accounting principles and appropriate accounting standards. Indeed, the nature of the standard setting process requires intensive interaction between the IASB and interested individuals and organizations from around the world. Powerful professional bodies, governments, and other stakeholders participate in the standard setting process and attempt to influence the direction and content of accounting standards by writing comment letters and heavily lobbying on the IASB (Larson 2007).

Secondly, companies in more than 115 countries are permitted to prepare financial information according to IFRS. These standards are principle-based and require the extensive application of professional judgments. Indeed, the IASB refers to the term 'substance over form' to highlight the importance of professional judgments for the interpretation and application of IFRS. This concept requires accountants to focus more on the economic substance of a business transaction than on its legal form. This is important if probability expressions have to be interpreted, materiality thresholds have to be assessed, and specific accounting policy options have to be selected. Probability expressions in particular are an important feature of principle-based standards such as IFRS, and are extensively used for the recognition, measurement, or disclosure of items. For example, International Accounting Standard[7] 18 (Revenue) requires revenue to be recognized "when it is *probable* that the economic benefits associated with the transaction will flow to the entity." (Paragraph 18, emphasis added). There is clear evidence that probability expressions are interpreted differently by accountants. Dimensions that may affect the quality of professional judgments include abilities motivation, confidence, risk attitude, cognitive style, gender, and cultural background (see Bonner 2008, for a discussion of these dimensions). For example, Doupnik and Richter (2004), who examined whether a common terminology may be interpreted differently across countries, found that German accountants interpret probability expressions more conservatively than their counterparts in

[7] IFRS issued until 2001 are called International Accounting Standards.

the United States. Additionally, Hellmann et al. (2010) found by interviewing German stakeholders that especially older accountants who have been using local accounting practices interpret IFRS using subliminal the local accounting principles. This is likely to cause issues of consistency in the interpretation and application of IFRS across countries.

Furthermore, companies may apply marketing techniques to influence the perception of annual report readers. For example, financial information is increasingly presented in form of pictures and graphs, and annual reports feature design elements such as headlines (Beattie and Jones 2008). This is becoming increasingly important with online financial reporting on corporate web sites. By using the emotive power of elements such as design, color and music in the context of the multi-dimensional possibilities of the internet, companies may have exponentially greater power to influence decision makers than in the two-dimensional format of the traditional annual report. The psychology literature provides evidence about framing effects in decision making. Specifically, there is clear evidence showing that the manner of information presentation or the way sentences are formulated are impacting decision making (for example Tversky & Kahneman 1981, Kahneman & Tversky 1984, Thaler 1980, Dunegan 1993, Gonzales et al. 2005, De Martino et al. 2006). A classic example is the *Asian Disease* problem developed by Tversky and Kahneman (1981). They took the same information and presented it differently to two groups of subjects. Subjects are informed about a disease that threatens 600 people and asked to choose between two options to combat the disease. In the positive frame, subjects were given the choice between saving 200 lives with certainty (option A), and a one-third chance that 600 people will be saved with a two-third chance of saving nobody (option B). In this group, most subjects prefer option A to option B. In the negative frame, subjects were asked to choose between 400 people dying with certainty (option C), and a two-third chance of 600 people dying and a one-third chance of nobody dying (option D). In this case most subjects preferred option D to option C, in spite of the fact that option A and option C are identical results, and option B and D are identical results (Tversky and Kahneman 1981). As such, they were able to demonstrate significant differences in choices across the two groups solely because of presentation differences. This reveals a tendency towards risk-aversion in human behavior. In other words, humans tend to be risk-averse if alternatives are related to gains, and select more often a risky alternative if alternatives are related to losses. This may be exploited by companies using the emotive power of design elements or rhetoric in their corporate communications. Similarly, information order may affect decisions

(Hogarth & Einhorn 1992). It is important to note that judgments of humans are not only limited by the information they possess but also by the timeframe that they have to process it and the amount of information they need to process. Related issues such as information overload have been discussed in chapter 1.

Thirdly, auditors are applying their professional judgments in order to verify the financial statements of a company. In other words, the same issues highlighted above may not only influence the preparation of financial statements but also their verification.

CONCLUSION

The *homo economicus* is a model which is extensively used to predict and explain economic phenomena. This model is based on two key characteristics of human behavior, namely selfishness and rationality. Mainstream accounting and finance literature is frequently referring to this model and is upholding an image of humans who make rational decisions by evaluating risks and returns of all alternatives. Behavioral finance criticizes the concept *of homo economicus* by highlighting that capital market participants are not always behaving rationally, are biased in their decisions, and apply a number of heuristics in order to develop their decisions. This chapter reviewed key heuristics of reasoning, namely the *representativeness heuristic, availability heuristic, anchoring-and-adjustment heuristic*, which are commonly used to explain biases in the psychology and behavioral economics literatures. The heuristics and biases outlined in this chapter provides clear evidence that (1) decisions are dependent on the presentation or formulation of the problem, (2) people are often risk-averse, (3) preferences are not stable, and (4) humans are not as selfish as the *homo economicus* model would predict. In short, it showed that the *homo economicus* model is too simplistic in its assumptions and that it is no longer sufficient in explaining the complexities that have emerged as a result of contextual advancements in society. This should be noted especially by researchers who still ground their research on theories that rely implicitly or explicitly on the *homo economicus*.

However, behavioral finance research would be too narrow if it focusses entirely on investors and other capital market participants. This chapter argues that the behavior of investors is greatly influenced by accounting information which is not neutral and value-free. It suggests that behavioral issues may arise on three dimensions, namely standard setting, preparation of financial information, and auditing. Behavioral aspects related to these three dimensions are important because they influence decisions of accountants who are ultimately responsible for providing the information that is the basis of their decisions. This is important to note for all stakeholders who use financial reporting for judgments and decisions, and who may believe that such quantitative information is more objective than actually is the case.

It is therefore essential that forthcoming paradigms incorporate behavioral aspects, as this will ensure relevance in explaining the intricacies of accounting and finance-related phenomena. This is particularly important in the accounting area because topics such as heuristics and biases have not received sufficient attention in this area (for example Bonner 2002008, p. 132).

The *homo economicus* model based on the rational behavior of users and their selfishness is too simplistic. It is high time that stakeholders move away from narrow approaches such as the *homo economicus* and develop new frameworks in accounting and finance, which focus on people and their behavior. The world is becoming more complex and simple answers are not suitable anymore. As Richard Thaler (2000, p. 140) eloquently predicts: "Homo economicus will evolve into homo sapiens".

ACKNOWLEDGMENT

The author is acknowledging the help of Chiing Yeow who wrote the appendix.

REFERENCES

Aspara, J., Tikkanen, H. (2008). Interactions of individuals' company-related attitudes and their buying of the companies' stocks and products. *Journal of Behavioral Finance*, 9(2), 85-94.

Barber, B.M., Odean, T. (2002). Online investors: do the slow die first?. *Review of Financial Studies*, 15, 455-488.

Beattie, V., Jones, M.J. (2008). Corporate reporting using graphs: A review and synthesis, *Journal of Accounting Literature*, 27(1), 71-110.

Benartzi, S. (2001). Excessive extrapolation and the allocation of 401(k) accounts to company stock. *Journal of Finance*, 56(5), 1747-1764.

Berg, J., Dickhaut, J., McCabe, K. (1995). Trust, reciprocity, and social history. *Games and Economic Behavior*, 10, 122-142.

Bonner, S. E. (2008). *Judgment and decision making in accounting*. Pearson Prentice Hall, New Jersey.

Bower, G.H. (1981). Mood and memory. *American Psychologist*, 36, 129-148.

Brown, C. (1981). Human information processing for decisions to investigate cost variances. *Journal of Accounting Research*, 19(1), 62-85.

Camerer, C.F. (1995). Individual decision making, in *Handbook of experimental economics*, J.H. Kagel, A.E. Roth, eds., Princeton University Press, Princeton.

Camerer, C.F., Fehr, E. (2006). When does the "economic man" dominate social behavior?. Science, 311(5757), 47-52.

Camerer, C.F., Loewenstein, G. (2004). Behavioral economics: Past, present and future, in *Advances in Behavioral Economics*, C.F. Camerer, G. Loewenstein, M. Rabin, eds., Princeton University Press, Princeton.

Chapman, G.B., Bornstein, B.H. (1996). The more you ask for, the more you get: Anchoring in personal injury verdicts. *Applied Cognitive Psychology*, 10, 519-540.

Cooper, A., Woo, C., Dunkelber, W. (1988). Entrepeneurs' perceived chances of success. *Journal of Business Venturing*, 3, 97-108.

De Bond, W. (2005). *The psychology of world equity markets*. Edward Elgar, Cheltenham.

De Bondt, W.F.M. (1998). A portrait of the individual investor. *European Economic Review*, 42, 831-844.

De Martino, B., Kumaran, D., Seymour, B., Dolan, R.J. (2006). Frames, biases, and rational decision-making in the human brain. *Science*, 313, 684-687.

Dohmen, T., Falk, A., Huffman, D., Uwe, S. (2009). Homo reciprocans: Survey evidence on behavioural outcomes. *Economic Journal*, 119(536), 592-612.

Doupnik, T. S., Richter, M. (2003). Interpretation of uncertainty expressions: a cross-national study. *Accounting, Organizations and Society*, 28(1), 15-35.

Doupnik, T. S., Richter, M. (2004). The impact of culture on the interpretation of "in text" verbal probability expressions. *Journal of International Accounting Research*, 3(1), 1-20.

Doupnik, T. S., Tsakumis, G.T. (2004). A critical review of tests of Gray's theory of cultural relevance and suggestions for future research. *Journal of Accounting Literature*, 23, 1-48.

Dunegan, K.J. (1993). Framing, cognitive modes, and image theory: Toward an understanding of a glass half full. *Journal of Applied Psychology,* 78(3), 491-503.

Englich, B., Mussweiler, T. (2001). Sentencing under uncertainty: Anchoring effects in the courtroom. *Journal of Applied Social Psychology*, 31, 1535-1551.

Faber, M., Peterson, T., Shiller, J. (2002). Homo oeconomicus and homo politicus in ecological economics. *Ecological Economics*, 4(3), 323-333.

Fehr, E., Gächter, S. (2000). Fairness and retaliation: The economics of reciprocity. Journal of Economic Perspectives, 14(3), 159-181.

Galinsky, A.D., Mussweiler, T. (2001). First officers as anchors: The role of perspective-taking and negotiator focus. *Journal of Personailty and Social Psychology*, 81, 657-669.

Gigerenzer, G., Goldstein, D.G. (1996). Reasoning the fast and frugal way: Models of bounded rationality. *Psychological Review*, 98, 506-528.

Gigerenzer, G., Czerlinski, J., Martignon, L. (2002). How good are fast and frugal heuristics?, in *Heuristics and biases: The psychology of intuitive judgment*, T. Gilovich, D. Griffin, D. Kahneman, eds., Cambridge University Press, Cambridge.

Gilovich, T., Griffin, D., Kahneman, D. (2002). *Heuristics and biases: The psychology of intuitive judgement.* Cambridge University Press, Cambridge.

Gonzales, C., Dana, J., Koshino, H., Just, M. (2005). The framing effect and risky decisions: Examining cognitive functions with fMRI. *Journal of Economic Psychology*, 26, 1-20.

Güth, W., Schmittberger, R., Schwarze, B. (1982) An experimental analysis of ultimatum bargaining. *Journal of Economic Behavior & Organization*, 3(4), 367-388.

Hardman, D. (2009). *Judgment and decision making: Psychological perspectives*. BPS Blackwell, West Sussex.

Häring, N., Storbeck, O. (2009). *Economics 2.0*. Palgrave MacMillan, New York.

Heinrich, J., Boyd, R., Bowels, S., Camerer, C., Fehr, E., Gintis, H., Mc Elreath, R. (2001). In search of homo economicus: Behavioral experiments in 15 small-scale societies. *American Economic Review*, 91(2), 73-78.

Hellmann, A., Perera, H., Patel, C. (2010). Contextual issues of the convergence of International Financial Reporting Standards: The case of

Germany, *Advances in Accounting, incorporating Advances in International Accounting*, 26(1), 108-116.

Hoffman, E., Mc Cabe, K., Smith, V. (1996). On expectations and monetary stakes in ultimatum games. *International Journal of Game Theory*, 25, 289-301.

Hogarth, R., Einhorn, H. (1992). Order effects in belief updating: The belief-adjustment model. *Cognitive Psychology*, (January 1992), 1-55.

Kahneman, D. (2003). Maps of bounded rationality: Psychology for behavioral economics. *American Economic Review*, 93(5), 14449-1475.

Kahneman, D., Frederick, S. (2002). Representativeness revisited: Attribute substituition in intuitive judgment, in *Heuristics and biases*, T. Gilovich, D. Griffin, D. Kahneman, eds., Cambridge University Press, Cambridge.

Kahneman, D., Tversky, A. (1972). Subjective probability: A judgment of representativenesss. *Cognitive Psychology*, 3, 430-454.

Kahneman, D., Tversky, A. (1973). On the psychology of prediction. *Psychological Review*, 80, 237-251.

Kahneman, D., Tversky, A. (1984). Choices, values, and frames. *American Psychologist*, 39(4), 341-350.

Kahneman, D., Tversky, A. (2000). *Choices, values and frames*. Cambridge University Press, Cambridge.

Koriat, A., Lichtenstein, S., Fischhoff, B. (1980). Reasons for confidence. *Journal of Experimental Psychology: Human Learning and Memory*, 6, 107-118.

Larson, R. K. (2007). Constituent Participation and the IASB's International Financial Reporting Interpretations Committee. *Accounting in Europe*, 4(2), 207-254.

Lichtenstein, S., Fischhoff, B., Phillips, L.D. (1982). Calibration of probabilities: The state of the art to 1980, in *Judgment under uncertainty: Heuristics and biases*. D. Kahneman, P. Slovic, A. Tversky, eds., Cambridge University Press, Cambridge.

List, J.A., Cherry, T.L. (2000). Learning to accept in ultimatum games: Evidence from and experimental design that generates low offers. *Experimental Economics*, 3, 11-31.

Massa, M., Simonov, A. (2006). Hedging, familiarity and portfolio choice. *The Review of Financial Studies*, 19(2), 633-685.

Merkl-Davies, D.M., Brennan, N.M. (2011). A conceptual framework of impression management: new insights from psychology, sociology and critical perspectives. *Accounting and Business Research*, 41(5), 415-437.

Mussweiler, T., Strack, F., Pfeiffer, T. (2000). Overcoming the inevitable anchoring effect: Considering the opposite compensates for selective accessibility. *Personality and Social Psychology Bulletin*, 26, 1142-1150.

Ng, I.C.L., Tseng, L. (2008). Learning to be sociable: The evolution of homo economicus. *American Journal of Economics and Sociology*, 67(2), 265-286.

Odean, T. (1999). Do investors trade too much?. *American Economic Review*, 89, 1279-1298.

Rausch, A. (2011). Reconstruction of decision-making behavior in shareholder and stakeholder theory: Implications for management accounting systems. *Review of Managerial Science*, 5(2-3), 137-169.

Rieskamp, J., Hertwig, R., Todd, P.M. (2006). Bounded rationality: Two interpretations from psychology, in *Handbook of Contemporary Cehavioral Economics: Foundations and Developments*, M. Altman, ed., Sharpe, New York.

Schneider, S. (2010). *Homo Oeconomicus oder doch eher Homer Simpson?*. Deutsche Bank Research, Frankfurt am Main.

Selten, R. (2001). What is bounded rationality?, in *Bounded rationality: The adaptive toolbax*, G. Gigerenzer, R. Selten, eds., MIT Press, Cambridge.

Shafir, E. (2004). *Preference, belief and similarity*. MIT Press, Cambridge.

Simon, H.A. (1957). Models of Man. Wiley, New York.

Thaler, R.H. (1980). Toward a positive theory of consumer choice. *Journal of Economic Behavior and Organization*, 1, 39-60.

Thaler, R.H. (2000). From homo economicus to homo sapiens. *Journal of Economic Perspectives*, 14(1), 133-141.

Todd, P., Gigerenzer, G. (2000). Precis of simple heuristics that make us smart. *Behavioral and Brain Science,* 23, 727-780.

Tversky, A., Kahneman, D. (1973). Availability: A heuristic for judging frequency and probability. *Cognitive Psychology*, 5, 207-232.

Tversky, A., Kahneman, D. (1974). Judgment under uncertainty: Heuristics and biases. *Science*, 185, 1124-1131.

Tversky, A., Kahneman, D. (1981). The framing of decisions and the psychology of choice. *Science*, 211, 453-458.

Tversky, A., Kahneman, D. (1983). Extensional versus intuitive reasoning: the conjunction fallacy in probability judgment. *Psychological Review*, 90, 292-315.

White, R., Hanson, D. (2000). Economic man and disciplinary boundaries: A case-study in corporate annual reports. *Accounting, Auditing & Accountability Journal*, 15(4), 450-477.

Wilkinson, N. (2008). *An introduction to behavioral economics*. Palgrave Macmillan, New York.

Wilson, T.D., Houston, C., Etling, K.M., Brekke, N. (1996). A new look at anchoring effects: Basic anchoring and its antecedents. *Journal of Experimental Psychology: General*, 4, 387-402.

Appendix: Refinements of the Homo Economicus Model

Due to anomalies discovered in the last decades, several refinements of the strict *homo economicus* model have been developed. In order to depict a more realistic paradigm, the *homo sociologicus*, for example, aims to integrate social norms into the strict model of selfish behavior. First proposed by Ralf Dahrendorf in 1958, the *homo sociologicus* recognizes that humans are not completely self-absorbed in nature and will have a tendency to act in the interest of others as well through acts of altruism. A characteristic of *homo sociologicus* is that his behavior is affected by social norms dictated through institutional policies, regulation, cultures, values and belief systems (Merkl-Davis & Brennan 2011). As such, he accounts for variables beyond the traditional utility function of *homo economicus*, and possesses emotional intellect and a sense of what is right and wrong. The major criticism of this concept is the explicit disregard of one's own self-interest (Ng & Tseng 2008). This suggests that the utility function is entirely influenced by variables which concern the wellbeing of others. The extremity of such behavior is rarely exhibited and unrealistic as it is unlikely that selfish behavior can be completely dismissed from the human psyche.

An alternative model which provides a more realistic variation of the *homo sociologicus* is the *homo reciprocans* whose actions are motivated by reciprocal fairness (Dohmen et al. 2009). Reciprocal fairness is derived from conformity to social norms and refers to the combination of being co-operative as well as willing to engage in punishment when unfairness disrupts the social norm. Reciprocal fairness is comprised of two parameters, namely positive reciprocity and negative reciprocity (Fehr & Gächter 2000). Positive reciprocity refers to the rewarding of co-operative tendencies, whereas negative reciprocity refers to the retaliatory tendencies and the willingness to punish (Fehr & Gächter 2000). *Homo reciprocans* has a behavioral propensity to vindicate unfairness, even to the extent that the punishment comes at a cost to them. This paradigm reflects a fundamental humanistic instinct of seeking justice and equity in a social environment. Social norms are specifically defined as a "behavioral regularity that is based on the normative preconception of how one ought to behave, which leads to the regulatory enforcement of the prescribed behavior through imposition of informal social sanctions" (Fehr & Gächter 2000, p. 854). As social norms influence behavior, *homo reciprocans* acts as a "norm enforcer" and is prescribed with a role which disciplines those who violate norms by acting egocentrically and defying the social status quo (Fehr & Gächter 2000).

Another variation is the *homo politicus* whose actions reflect the public interest and is governed by the ideologies of seeking political justice in a political environment. Political justice refers to the general consensus of a community and is particularly concerned with what is regarded best in the public's interest (Faber et al. 2002). *Homo politicus* encompasses moral intuition and interprets social issues as comprised of rights and obligations. The notion of political justice takes into consideration issues such as sustainability and involves the long-term repercussions of present-day decisions as the common good is defined as being what is best for generations to come. This suggests that *homo politicus* focuses on long-term decision making. As *homo politicus* strives for the good of the community, there is an implied desire to receive approval from others for his actions and behavior. Consequently, he has intentions of acquiring political power by persuading others of his view and seeking their consent (Faber et al. 2002). This paradigm is associated with public choice theory as well as the regulatory capture theory. These theories articulate the context in which the *homo politicus* exists.

In: Behavioral Accounting
Editor: Andreas Hellmann
ISBN: 978-1-62618-039-0
© 2013 Nova Science Publishers, Inc.

Chapter 3

ENFORCEMENT AND MANAGERS' FINANCIAL REPORTING BEHAVIOR: A REVIEW OF THE EMPIRICAL ENFORCEMENT LITERATURE

Brigitte Eierle *** and Miriam Schleicher***
University of Bamberg, Germany

ABSTRACT

Due to agency problems and contractual agreements managers have an incentive to manipulate the financial accounting information of their companies. Therefore, to ensure high-quality financial reports effective enforcement mechanisms are considered crucial. We provide a framework for analyzing the impact of enforcement actions on management`s accounting behavior and review current empirical research in this area. Specifically we assess research on sanctions imposed on managers by companies for fraudulent accounting behavior and the (deterrent) effect of enforcement on managers' earnings management and disclosure behavior. Our literature review concludes that current research has generated useful insights into the relationship between enforcement and management's accounting behavior. However, we also identify several areas of interest that have not been adequately addressed in research yet, and show that changes in the enforcement environment

---

* Tel: +49(0)951/863-2545. E-mail: brigitte.eierle@uni-bamberg.de.

following financial reporting scandals raise the demand for updated research.

1. Introduction

Since the Enron scandal in 2000, accounting fraud cases have increased in the last years (Ernst and Young 2010). Therefore not only the issue of accounting fraud but also discussions on the financial reporting behavior of managers has largely grown in the accounting literature. By committing accounting fraud the behavior of the manager is influenced by "the intentional deception of another person by lying and cheating for the purpose of deriving an unjust economic advantage over that person" (Bologna 1984). The fraudulent financial reporting behavior of a manager can span from manipulating accounting documents, excluding relevant and material accounting information, the recognition of non-existing transactions, the incorrect application of accounting standards to the incomplete disclosure of relevant accounting information (Riahi-Belkaoui 2004). The SEC concludes that "[c]onsistent and high-quality implementation is necessary for investors to benefit from a set of high-quality global accounting standards" (SEC Release Nos. 33-9109, 34-61578, p. 18). Thus, effective enforcement mechanisms are considered crucial for high-quality financial reports. Enforcement can be regarded as a three-part process consisting of an efficient control system and management, an effective audit by independent auditors and an oversight mechanism with sufficient expertise and power to ensure effective enforcement (Brown and Tarca 2005). The literature documents several investigations providing evidence that with the failure of one part of this three-part enforcement process, fraudulent reporting will exist. For example Ashbaugh-Skaife et al. (2008) show that without an effective internal control system, there is less financial reporting reliability. Francis (2004) demonstrates that high audit quality represented by Big Five auditors can diminish accounting fraud and Brown and Tarca (2005) point out that an oversight mechanism is necessary to curb accounting fraud. However, despite the general agreement that effective enforcement mechanisms are necessary to ensure high quality financial reporting, enforcement structures differ extremely across countries.

Due to these structural differences in enforcement systems across jurisdictions, the deterrent effect of enforcement on management`s fraudulent behavior may differ from country to country.

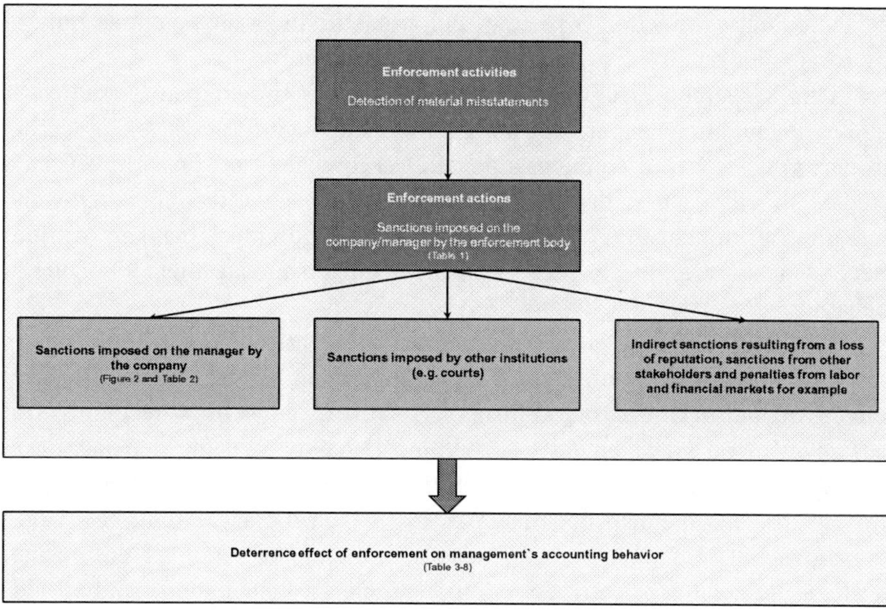

Figure 1. Framework for analyzing the effect of enforcement actions on management behavior.

In this paper we review the empirical literature dealing with the impact of enforcement on management behavior. Thereby we specifically focus on institutional oversight mechanisms responsible for enforcing financial reporting requirements (enforcement bodies). We argue that enforcement activities from enforcement bodies result in deterrent effects thereby influencing managers' financial reporting behavior (figure 1).

Using the framework provided in figure 1 our paper is organized as follows. Section 2 analyses the demand for enforcement and provides an overview of the major features of enforcement bodies from different countries. We argue that the demand for an effective enforcement is caused by agency problems. Thus, the quality of financial reports can be improved by effective enforcement mechanisms due to the incentive (deterrent effects) it provides for the management. Our analysis shows however, that there are substantial differences between enforcement bodies across countries, especially with regard to audit regularity and available sanctions. Accordingly, the deterrence effect and therefore the effectiveness of enforcement activities may vary across countries. Section 3 reviews empirical findings on sanctions imposed by companies on directors after enforcement actions.[1]

This research documents, that managers from companies subject to enforcement actions experience a higher management turnover and a decrease in performance based compensation after enforcement actions. However, the studies in this section do not investigate cause and effect for single units making any conclusions on causal effects for individual mangers difficult. Section 4 analyzes the impact of enforcement on management`s accounting behavior.

Research findings provide evidence that earnings management and disclosure quality are influenced by enforcement confirming the deterrent effect of enforcement mechanisms. However, the effect resulting from enforcement on management's accounting behavior strongly depends on the strength of the enforcement system in place. We therefore can infer from our review that enforcement does have an impact on the accounting behavior of managers but that due to differences across countries not all enforcement systems are equally effective. Section 5 summarizes our findings and provides some conclusions for future research.

2. The Demand for Enforcement in Financial Reporting

In this section we investigate the demand for an effective enforcement system in financial reporting. Principal agent conflicts and performance based compensation contracts may motivate the manager to provide untruthful financial reports.

Enforcement actions are one solution to mitigate these problems by disciplining managers for fraudulent reporting and providing deterrent effects on other managers.

[1] Sanctions imposed by other institutions (e.g. national legislators) and indirect sanctions are not within the scope of our literature review. For research on capital market responses following enforcement actions see for example Nourayi (1994); Anderson and Yohn (2002); Wu (2002); Muradoglu and Huskey (2008); Karpoff et al. (2008b); Wang and Yu (2009); Christensen et al. (2011); Leng et al. (2011); Hribar and Jenkins (2004); Hail and Leuz (2006); Kim and Shi (2007); Li (2010). For labor market penalties see for example Desai et al. 2006 and Collins et al. 2009.

2.1. Agency Problem

Due to information asymmetries and conflicts of interest principal agent conflicts arise between managers and contracting partners (e.g. lenders and other creditors), that is between managers (agent) and owners (principals) and/or between managers acting in the interest of owners (agent) and other contracting partners (principals) (Wagenhofer and Ewert 2003). This creates a demand for financial reporting. First, contracting partners need financial information for their resource allocation decisions since managers have substantial information available that is not directly accessible to outsiders. Second, contracting partners need information to evaluate and control the management's economic behavior since the actions of the management are not directly observable and it cannot be expected to act in the contracting partners' best interest (Gjesdal 1981). But since managers will anticipate the way they are evaluated, any accounting information used to control the management in turn provides incentives to manipulate financial reporting data. Furthermore, contractual agreements suggested for mitigating principal agent conflicts by aligning the interests of managers with those of external business partners suffer from similar problems. Such contracts also require information that enables external contracting partners to monitor managers' compliance with the contractual agreements thereby providing incentives to manipulate the relevant data (Gjesdal 1981). One solution to this problem is to require an audit for the financial data that need to be reported by the management. This however may lead to further principal agent conflicts between the auditor (agent) and the contracting partners (principals) requiring the audit (Gjesdal 1981). Due to these multiple principal agent conflicts an independent accounting enforcement system is considered necessary to assure truthful financial reporting.

An independent enforcement mechanism has two major effects on management behavior: First, enforcement has a disciplinary effect by sanctioning the manager for fraudulent reporting behavior. Thereby sanctions for fraudulent behavior can be imposed directly on the manager by the enforcement body itself and/or by other institutions (e.g. courts or company's governance bodies). Furthermore, indirect sanctions may result from a loss of reputation, sanctions from other stakeholders as well as via disciplining measures from labor and financial markets for example. Second, enforcement actions have a deterrent effect on other managers keeping them from engaging in untruthful financial reporting behavior by threatening them with sanctions and loss of reputation. Finally, enforcement also strengthens the position of the auditor if there are disagreements between the management and the auditor regarding truthful accounting policies.

In our literature review we assess the disciplinary effect of enforcement as well as the deterrent effect of enforcement by reviewing the empirical literature on (1) sanctions imposed on managers by companies after enforcement actions and (2) the impact of enforcement systems on mangers' earnings management and disclosure behavior.

2.2. Cross Country Differences Regarding the Features of Enforcement Bodies

Enforcement is defined as "monitoring compliance of the financial information with the applicable reporting framework; taking appropriate measures in case of infringements discovered in the course of enforcement" (Committee of European Securities Regulators 2003). It can be seen as a three-part process consisting of an effective control system and management, independent auditors who are experts in the accounting rules and an oversight mechanism with sufficient expertise and power to obtain effective enforcement (Brown and Tarca 2005).[2] However focusing on the latter, national enforcement bodies vary across countries not only with respect to their structure and organization but also with respect to their competencies, enforcement procedures and sanction mechanisms.

According to the Committee of European Securities Regulators (2003) an institutional oversight mechanism should be a competent independent administrative authority which is set up by member states to be responsible for enforcement. However, in Europe there are currently five different approaches to regulate financial reporting enforcement, namely enforcement by stock exchanges, by a regulator of a stock exchange, by a separate private review panel, by a separate governmental body, and no institutional financial reporting oversight at all (Fédération des Experts Comptables Européens 2001). As a consequence, the different types of enforcement bodies have different competencies (e.g. with respect to engage in pre-clearance activities), enforcement procedures (e.g. regarding the access to internal accounting material or the frequency with which an audit is conducted) and sanction

[2] Our literature refers to enforcement activities of accounting enforcement bodies only. Other enforcement activities such as legal enforcement by courts, or enforcement by a company's governance bodies as well as enforcement by auditors are out of the scope of this paper.

mechanisms (e.g. power to impose fines or require the delisting of a company). For example, the audit frequency as enforcement procedure varies from every year in France to every four to five years in Germany. Sanction mechanisms available to European enforcement bodies range from publishing the detected accounting irregularities to imposing fines, referring the cases to courts or to require the delisting of a company. Enforcement bodies in other countries, like for example the SEC in the USA, even have the power to require companies to restate their financial statements.

Due to differences in the institutional environment accounting literature often distinguishes between common law enforcement and code law enforcement (La Porta et al. 1997; Ball et al. 2000). While enforcement in common law countries has traditionally been a private matter including civil litigation enforcement in code law countries is historically within the responsibility of governance bodies requiring administrative agencies to prosecute code violations (Ball et al. 2000, for further differences between code law and common law countries with respect to financial reporting see Nobes and Parker 2008). Table 1 gives an overview of the primary features of major enforcement bodies in the world revealing the differences that currently exist between enforcement institutions across countries.

Since the organization, competencies, enforcement procedures and sanctions of enforcement bodies vary across jurisdictions enforcement mechanisms may not be equally effective in all countries. Therefore, significant research exists assessing the consequences of enforcement actions for the management and the impact of enforcement on managers' accounting behavior.

Table 1. Features of major enforcement bodies

Country		Enforcement body	Oversight type	Sanction mechanism					Audit frequency
				Public statement	Imposing fines	Referring to court	Restate-ment	Delisting	
Code law countries	China	CSRC	Government body	X	X	X		X	Information not available
	France	COB	Stock exchange regulator	X	X	X		X	Voluntary every year
	Germany	FREP/BaFin	Review panel and government body	X	X	X			Every four to five years
Common law countries	Australia	ASIC	Government body	X	X	X			At least every four years
	U.K.	FRRP	Review panel	X		X			Matters drawn to its intention
	USA	SEC	Stock exchange regulator	X	X	X	X	X	Every three years

Table 2. Studies analyzing the consequences companies take to sanction managers' untruthful financial reporting

		Years analyzed	Topic analyzed
USA	Collins et al. (2005)	1997 to 2002	▪ CEO- and other top executive-turnover ▪ CEO and other top executives` bonus compensation
	Arthaud-Day et al. (2006)	1997 to 2002	CEO- and CFO-turnover
	Desai et al. (2006)	1997 to 2002	Other top executive-turnover
	Cheng & Farber (2008)	1997 to 2001	Managers` option based compensation
	Hennes et al. (2008)	2002 to 2006	CEO- and CFO-turnover
	Karpoff et al. (2008)	1977 to 2006	CEO- and other top executive-turnover
	Agrawal & Cooper (2009)	1997 to 2002	CEO- and other top executive-turnover
	Collins et al. (2009)	1997 to 2006	▪ CFO-turnover ▪ CFO salary
	Wang & Chou (2011)	2002 to 2005	CEO- and CFO-turnover
China	Chen et al. (2005)	1999 to 2003	CEO-turnover
	Sun & Zhang (2006)	1990 to 2002	CEO-turnover

3. Sanctions from Companies for Managers after Enforcement Actions

If accounting irregularities are detected by an institutional enforcement body an enforcement action[3] will be originated. Since enforcement actions are costly to the company increasing for example the risk of litigation and a loss in the company's market value (Cheng and Farber 2008) companies may impose sanctions on managers detected by enforcement bodies for untruthful reporting.

For example, companies can sanction the fraudulent accounting behavior by replacing the manager responsible for the accounting misstatement or by changing his/her compensation scheme. Studies analyzing the consequences companies take to sanction managers' fraudulent financial reporting are presented in table 2.

[3] An enforcement action is the result of an investigation by an enforcement institution which results in sanction mechanisms (Committee of European Securities Regulators 2003).

3.1. Replacement of Managers

Provided that the internal governance mechanisms are effective enough to identify the managers responsible for the misreporting and the benefits from replacing the manager are higher than the costs for substituting the manager's firm-specific knowledge, it is likely that the manager will be dismissed after an enforcement action.

Consistent with this reasoning several studies adduce evidence for the US that the executive- (CEO, CFO, COO, Executive Vice President) turnover has increased after a restatement (see for CEO-turnover figure 2).[4] Collins et al. (2005) find that compared to non-event years the rate of the turnover for CEOs and other top executives is higher in those years where irregularities were detected by the SEC and restatements had to be made by the company. Arthaud-Day et al. (2006) and Wang and Chou (2011) show for CEOs and CFOs, Desai et al. (2006) as well as Agrawal and Cooper (2009) for CEOs and other top executives (chairman, CEO and/or president) as well as Collins et al. (2009) for CFOs a higher turnover rate in the first two years after the announcement of a restatement.

Thereby Agrawal and Cooper (2009) are able to provide evidence that turnover rates are even larger for restatements that are more severe, cause greater decreases in stock prices or result in negative earnings restatements.[5] Furthermore, Collins et al. (2009) as well as Wang and Chou (2011) report higher turnover rates after restatements for periods after 2002, that is when the Sarbanes-Oxley Act (SOX) has been in force, compared to pre-SOX periods. Hennes et al. (2008) as well as Leone and Liu (2010) demonstrate a higher CEO- and CFO-turnover rate between six months before and six months after the announcement of a restatement.

Thereby Hennes et al. (2008) find out that CEO- and CFO-turnover rates are higher for parent-level managers responsible for parent-level restatements than for subsidiary-level managers accountable for subsidiary-level restatements. Leone and Liu (2010) report higher CFO-turnover rates and

---

4 Some studies also investigate the turnover rate of audit committee members (e.g. Srinivasan 2005; Arthaud-Day 2006), outside directors (e.g. Srinivasan 2005) and auditors (e.g. Agrawal and Cooper 2009). The findings of these studies are not included in our literature review since our paper focuses on management behavior. In addition we also excluded studies that do not specifically focus on accounting fraud detected by an enforcement body but examine management-turnover caused by revelation of lawsuits and fraud in general (e.g. Persons 2006; Agrawal et al. 1999).

5 In addition, Desai et al. (2006) show that only 15% of the managers replaced after an enforcement action were rehired at a similar position after their dismissal.

lower CEO-turnover rates after enforcement actions if the CEO is also the founder of the company indicating that the CFO is more likely to be held responsible for misreporting if the CEO is the founder of the company. Karpoff et al. (2008a) examine the turnover rate for CEOs and other top executives after SEC and DOJ (Department of Justice) enforcement actions (including administrative, civil and criminal proceedings) for financial misrepresentations.

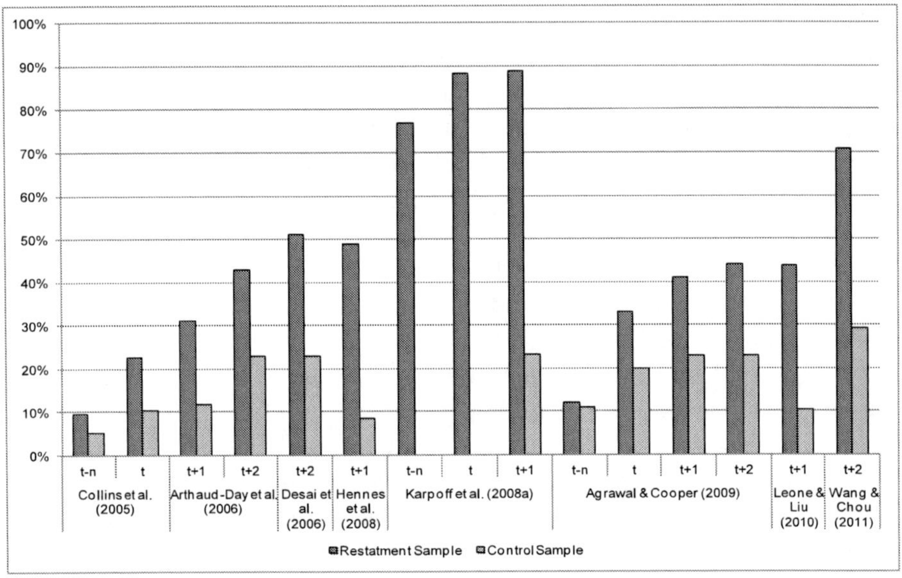

Figure 2. Probability of CEO-turnover after an enforcement action in the US.

They supplement findings from previous studies and find a higher turnover rate after enforcement actions for the time period beginning with the accounting violation and ending 90 days after the enforcement period. Finally Chen et al. (2005) as well as Sun and Zhang (2006) investigate the CEO-turnover rate for China after an enforcement action by the China Securities Regulatory Commission (CSRC). Similar to the findings from studies for US companies Chen et al. (2005) report for the year before and after the enforcement action and Sun and Zhang (2006) for two years after the enforcement action a higher CEO-turnover rate for the firms subject to a CSRC enforcement action.

In summary, research from the US and China provides evidence that turnover rates for executives are higher for companies subject to an enforcement action compared to a control sample of companies with no enforcement actions. So far there are only studies for the US and China available raising the question to which extent the findings from this research can be transferred to other countries with different governance structures. In addition, the research results suffer from several limitations. First, some studies include all restatements that are publicly available (e.g. Collins et al. 2009; Wang et al. 2010) in their analysis without distinguishing between restatements resulting from unintentional misapplications of accounting standards (accounting error) and intentional misreporting (accounting irregularity). Since sanctions for intentional misreporting are likely to be more severe than those for unintentional misapplications of accounting standards inferences drawn from research results that do not distinguish between these two sources of misstatements may be misleading as shown by Hennes et al. (2008). Second, difficulties arise to distinguish between restatement related and non-restatement related leaves. Only very few studies analyzing the management turnover after enforcement actions (e.g. Wang et al. 2010) differentiate with respect to their management turnover figure between managers that leave the company voluntarily and managers that are dismissed by the company. However, only the latter are relevant for researching the sanctions resulting from enforcement actions.

Therefore, research findings that mingle restatement related with voluntary turnover can lead to misinterpretations regarding the effectiveness of sanctions mechanisms. Third, in the US restatements can be prompted by the company itself, the company's auditors or the SEC. To draw conclusions whether an enforcement action from an enforcement body causes sanctions from a company only restatements required by the enforcement body itself are relevant.

Therefore, any studies that do not clearly differentiate between these different types of restatements (e.g. Collins et al. 2005; Leone and Liu 2010; Wang et al. 2010) may restrict conclusions on the consequences managers experience after enforcement actions. Finally, none of the studies investigate cause and effect for single units and therefore limit conclusions on causal effects for individual managers.

Thus, the findings on higher turnover rates for managers after enforcement actions do not necessarily imply that actually those managers responsible for the untruthful reporting were dismissed by the company as a consequence for their misreporting behavior.

3.2. Changes in Management's Compensation Contracts

In principal agent settings performance based compensation schemes are often used to align the interest of managers with those of the owners. However, "bonus schemes create incentives for managers to select accounting procedures and accruals to maximize the value of their bonus awards" (Healy 1985: 106). Research documents a link between equity based compensation and financial reporting failures (Efendi et al. 2007; Burns and Kedia 2006; Armstrong et al. 2010). Consequently, if material misstatements are detected by enforcement bodies indicating that managers manipulated financial accounting data for their own wealth maximization the contractual agreements are usually revisited by the company's governance bodies. Therefore, besides the literature on management-turnover there are a few studies available investigating the re-contracting of managers' compensation schemes after financial reporting failure.[6]

Collins et al. (2005) provide evidence that CEOs and other top executives experience a bonus penalty in the year the accounting irregularities were detected by the SEC and in the year the restatement had to be issued. However, they also demonstrate that restatements do not significantly impact the total compensation of CEOs and other top executives (Collins et al. 2005). Cheng and Farber (2008) investigate the change in option-based compensation within two years after the announcement of a restatement. They supplement the findings from Collins et al. (2005) showing that managers of companies filing a restatement experience a decrease of 6% in their option-based compensation which is significantly different to the control sample reporting an increase by 3% for the same time period. Reductions in the option-based proportion of total compensation are reported for extant as well as for newly hired managers.

In summary, there are only very few studies assessing the impact of enforcement actions on managers' compensation. The studies available provide evidence that companies reduce the performance based compensation of their top executives after accounting failures. These findings suggest that re-negotiations of compensation schemes after financial misreporting primarily are used to decrease management's incentives for untruthful reporting. Since only studies from the US are available assessing the re-contracting of managers' compensation plans after accounting failure it remains uncertain

[6] There are also studies examining labor market penalties for managers that were displaced after financial reporting failures (see Fn. 1) which are however beyond the scope of our paper.

whether these findings apply to other countries as well. In addition, the research presented in this section suffers from similar limitations as the studies discussed in section 3.1. First, generally, the compensation of executives consists of different elements: fixed basic salaries, bonus, stock options, restricted stock and other long-term incentives. In order to get a comprehensive picture on the re-contracting activities of companies after misreporting all of these elements should be assessed which however is not done by any of the studies above. Second, since managers' intention for misreporting is not observable it is challenging to distinguish between intentional misreporting and unintentional application of accounting standards. For studies that fail to differentiate between the causes for enforcement actions it is difficult to attribute the re-contracting activities to agency problems and managers' intentional misreporting behavior. Third, none of the studies distinguishes between company-, auditor- or SEC-prompted restatements. For any conclusions on the consequences a manager experiences after an enforcement action from the enforcement body only restatements prompted by the enforcement body itself are relevant. Finally, none of the studies assess causal effects for individual managers. Therefore, there still are important gaps in our knowledge to what extend re-contracting of compensation schemes is used to penalize managers accountable for accounting failures and to what extent companies generally adjust their executive compensation schemes after misreporting to mitigate their agency problems.

4. Impact of Enforcement on Management`s Financial Reporting Behavior

Enforcement actions are costly to managers (Cheng and Farber 2008). Literature documents that managers accountable for fraudulent reporting experience various sanctions (loss of reputation, fines from enforcement bodies, displacements, decreases in performance based compensations, labor market penalties etc., see for example Karpoff and Lott 1993; Brown and Tarca 2005; Desai et al. 2006; Cheng and Farber 2008; Collins et al. 2009). Anticipating the negative effects of misreporting enforcement mechanisms provide deterrent effects on managers. For managers' decisions whether to engage in intentional misreporting or not the benefits from misreporting will be weighed against the expected sanctions. Therefore, the deterrent effect of an enforcement system largely depends on its features (e.g. the audit frequency influencing the probability of being detected for an accounting fraud) and subsequent sanctions for reporting infringements. For this reason a large branch of literature examines the impact of enforcement on managements' accounting behavior providing evidence on the deterrent effect of enforcement systems.[7]

4.1. Impact on Earnings Management

Applying accounting standards requires judgment and therefore offers managers discretion to manage reported earnings to benefit themselves. Therefore, the more flexible the standards are the more non-abused accounting earnings management is possible. However, managers cannot only manage earnings the way accounting standards are applied but also by deciding on the timing and/or structuring of real transactions (e.g. decisions on inventory levels, to defer RandD expenditures or how to structure leasing contracts) (Ewert and Wagenhofer 2005, Healy and Wahlen 1999). Accordingly, "Earnings management occurs when managers use judgment in financial reporting and in structuring transactions to alter financial reports to either mislead some stakeholders about the underlying economic performance of the company or to influence contractual outcomes that depend on reported accounting numbers" (Healy and Wahlen 1999: 368). By monitoring compliance with applicable accounting standards and providing appropriate sanction mechanisms enforcement can impact accounting earnings misrepresentations. However, enforcement can only impact abused discretion afforded by accounting standards. Earnings management caused by timing/structuring real transactions (real earnings management) as well as the management of accounting earnings within the discretion offered by accounting standards are beyond the scope of enforcement activities even though they may have a negative impact on agency costs.

Therefore, enforcement can influence earnings management only to the extent accounting rules are abused. The deterrent effect of an enforcement system largely depends on its effectiveness. Thus, earnings management is expected to be lower if an adequate enforcement mechanism is in place that effectively protects outsider interests (Leuz et al. 2003).

---

[7] There are also studies examining capital market responses following enforcement actions or labor market penalties for managers (see Fn. 1) which are not part of this literature review.

Table 3. Earnings management measurements

		Measurement							
		Dechow et al. (1995)	Basu (1997)	Burgstahler & Dichev (1997)	Skinner & Myers (1999)	Dechow & Skinner (2000)	DeFond & Park (2001)	Dechow & Dichev (2002)	Larcker & Richardson (2004)
Study	Ball et al. (2000)		X						
	Leuz et al. (2003)	X		X	X	X			
	Burgstahler et al. (2006)	X		X	X	X			
	Lang et al. (2006)			X					
	Cai et al. (2008)	X				X			
	Callao & Jarne (2010)								X
	Böcking et al. (2012)	X							
	Ernstberger et al (2012)						X	X	

Table 4. Proxies for measuring the strength of enforcement in cross country studies assessing earnings management behavior

		Model	Measurement
Study	Ball et al. (2000)	David and Brierley (1985)	• Code law enforcement • Common law enforcement
	Leuz et al. (2003)	La Porta et al. (1998)	Mean score across: • legal system efficiency • rule of law • corruption index
	Burgstahler et al. (2006)	La Porta et al. (1998)	Mean score across: • legal system efficiency • rule of law • corruption index
	Lang et al. (2006)	La Porta et al. (1998)	Level of investor protection based on the outside investor rights
	Cai et al. (2008)	• La Porta et al. (1998) • Beny (2005)	Mean score across: • legal system efficiency • rule of law • corruption index • insider trading laws index
	Callao & Jarne (2010)	La Porta et al. (1998)	Mean score across: • legal system efficiency • rule of law • corruption index

Against this background, several studies assess the link between enforcement and earnings management. Since it is impossible to directly observe how managers apply discretion to manage earnings various measurement proxies were developed for measuring earnings management and were used in research studies (see table 3).

The studies analyzing the impact of enforcement mechanisms on earnings management can be divided into two categories: cross country and single country studies. While cross country studies compare the effectiveness of different enforcement mechanisms across different countries single country studies only analyze one country and the effectiveness of its enforcement system. As proxy for the strength of the enforcement system in a country most cross country studies use some of the enforcement measures compiled by La Porta et al. (1998). La Porta et al. (1998) provide proxies for the quality of enforcement systems using scores collected by private credit risk agencies for the use of foreign investors. Most commonly the strength of enforcement is measured by the mean score across following variables from La Porta et al. (1998): (1) "efficiency of the judicial system" – score provided by the country risk rating agency Business International Corp. measuring the efficiency and integrity of the legal environment of a country; (2) "rule of law" – score provided by the International Country Risk guide measuring the law and order tradition in a country; and, (3) "corruption" – score provided by the International Country Risk guide measuring the corruption in government (for more detailed definitions of these three variables see La Porta et al. 1998). Some researchers extend the enforcement proxy described above by including further variables (such as scores for insider trading laws) in their enforcement measurement; others rely on a single variable for their enforcement measurement (see table 4). Comparing the enforcement scores presented by La Porta et al. (1998) it appears that common law countries display higher scores than countries with a code law tradition indicating generally a weaker enforcement for the latter (La Porta et al. 1998). Therefore, studies often include the country's legal origin as an additional variable in their models or solely rely on a distinction between code law and common law to measure the strength of an enforcement system (see table 4).

There are numerous studies assessing the relationship between earnings management and enforcement quality (see table 5). Leuz et al. (2003), Cai et al. (2008) and Ball et al. (2000) report for an international sample of countries and Burgstahler et al. (2006) as well as Callao and Jarne (2010) for a sample of European countries a negative association between earnings management and the strength of enforcement. Leuz et al. (2003) distinguish in their study between outsider economies with large stock markets, dispersed ownerships, strong investor protection rights and strong enforcement (such as the US), insider economies with less-developed stock markets, concentrated ownership, weak investor protection rights and strong enforcement (such as Germany) and insider economies with weak enforcement (such as Thailand) and show that insider economies with weak enforcement reveal higher levels of earnings management than outsider economies with strong enforcement. Supporting the results of Leuz et al. (2003), Ball et al. (2000) and Cai et al. (2008) find that companies in the US, Canada and Australia exhibiting high enforcement scores show the lowest level of earnings management while countries such as the Philippines, Germany or Japan with low enforcement scores exhibit higher degrees of earnings management. Burgstahler et al. (2006) report higher earnings management scores in companies with German legal origin than in companies with English, Scandinavian or French legal origin supporting the hypothesis that earnings management is higher in countries with weaker legal systems and enforcement. Additional they find that publicly traded companies in countries with high enforcement scores show the lowest level of earnings management whereas privately held companies in countries with low enforcement scores have the highest level of earnings management. Consistent with Burgstahler et al. (2006), Callao and Jarne (2010) show that strong enforcement diminishes earnings management. By comparing financial reporting data from US listed companies with Non-US companies cross listed in the US Lang et al. (2006) show higher degrees of earnings management in the cross listed companies which are in practice not as strictly enforced by the SEC as US firms (Siegel 2005). These findings confirm results from other studies providing evidence that a strong enforcement mitigates earnings management. Finally Ernstberger et al. (2012) as well as Böcking et al. (2012) investigate in a single country study for Germany the influence of the enforcement system on the degree of earnings management. While Ernstberger et al. (2012) report a decrease in the level of earnings management after German enforcement reforms Böcking et al. (2012) provide evidence that companies with enforcement error announcements show higher levels of earnings management in the year after an investigation by the German enforcement body (FREP/BaFin).The findings from Böcking et al. (2012) indicate that managers seem to "feel save" in the year after the error announcement and do not expect to be investigated immediately after an assessment in the previous year. Accordingly, earnings management is only reduced if enforcement features (regularity of investigations, sanctions, etc.) provide a sufficient deterrent effect.

In summary, the evidence from the earnings management literature indicates that strong enforcement can mitigate earnings management. However, since enforcement features vary extremely across countries (see section 2) not all enforcement systems are equally effective as shown by the research results above.

Table 5. Impact of enforcement actions on earnings management

		Measurement	Years analyzed	Countries analyzed	Findings: Impact of enforcement on earnings management
Cross country study	Ball et al. (2000)	Code law enforcement vs. Common law enforcement	1985 to 1995	France	~
				Germany	~
				Japan	~
				Australia	-
				Canada	-
				U.K.	~
				USA	-
	Leuz et al. (2003)	Score	1990 to 1999	Norway, Australia, Canada, Hong Kong, Malaysia, Singapore, USA	-
				Austria, Belgium, Denmark, Finland, France, Germany, Japan, Netherlands, Sweden, Switzerland, Taiwan, Ireland, South Africa	~
				Indonesia, Italy, Philippines, Portugal, South Korea, Spain, India, Pakistan, Thailand	~
	Burgstahler et al. (2006)	Score	1997 to 2003	Austria, Germany	~
				Belgium, France, Greece, Italy, Netherlands, Portugal, Spain	-
				Denmark, Finland, Sweden	-
				U.K.	-
	Lang et al. (2006)	Level of investor protection	1991 to 2002	Argentina, Brazil, Chile, China, Denmark, Dominican Republic, Finland, France, Germany, Greece, Hungary, Italy, Japan, Mexico, Netherlands, Norway, eru, Philippines, Portugal, South Korea, Spain, Sweden, Switzerland, Taiwan, Venezuela, Australia, Hong Kong, Ghana, Ireland, Israel, New Zealand, Singapore, South Africa, U.K.	-
	Cai et al. (2008)	Score	2000 to 2006	Austria, Belgium, Denmark, Finland, France, Germany, Greece, Indonesia, Italy, Japan, Netherlands, Norway, Philippines, Portugal, South Korea, Spain, Sweden, Switzerland, Taiwan, Australia, Canada, Hong Kong, India, Ireland, Malaysia, New Zealand, Pakistan, Singapore, South Africa, Thailand, U.K., USA	-
	Callao & Jame (2010)	Score	1997 to 2006	Belgium, Finland, France, Germany, Italy, Netherlands, Portugal, Spain, Sweden	-
Single country study	Böcking et al. (2012)	-	2005 to 2009	Germany	~
	Ernstberger et al. (2012)	-	2003 to 2006	Germany	-

Key:
- means that enforcement negatively influences the extent of earnings management
~ means that there is no impact of enforcement on earnings management

There are some limitations concerning the conclusions that can be drawn on enforcement bodies from the studies on earnings management. First, a major limitation results from the difficulties to measure earnings management. Since it is a problem to distinguish in empirical studies between real earnings management, earnings management without abusing applicable accounting standards and abused earnings manipulations, with only the latter being subject to enforcement actions by accounting enforcement bodies, the results on the impact of regulatory enforcement features on earnings management may be biased (similar Ewert and Wagenhofer 2005). Second, there are difficulties to measure the quality of a country's enforcement system.

Table 6. Measurement of disclosure quality

		Measurement
Cross country study	Hope (2003)	Assessment based on a checklist with 144 items for US-GAAP and 153 items for IFRS annual report disclosures including the following topics: • general information • income statement • balance sheet • funds/cash flow statements • accounting policies • stockholder's information • supplementary information
Cross country study	Aerts & Tarca (2010)	Assessment according to a checklist measuring the following: • density of explanations • depth of explanations • valence inconsistency in formality • valence inconsistency in depth • technical-accounting explanations • informality bias on positives • assertive causal bias • use of entitlements and enhancements • defensive causal bias • use of excuses, justifications and causality denials
Single country study	Glaum & Street (2003)	Assessment based on a checklist with 144 items for US-GAAP and 153 items for IFRS annual report disclosures including the following topics: • revenue recognition • consolidated financial statements • equity accounting • business combinations • goodwill • foreign currency translation • intangible assets • property, plant and equipment • impairment • capitalization of interest cost • research and development • investments • financial instruments • inventory • leasing • capital intruments and debt • taxation • provisions and contingencies • shareholder's equity • employee share option plans • pension costs and post retirement benefits other than pensions • reporting financial performance • earnings per share • cash flow statements • segment reporting • post balance sheet events

Therefore, all cross studies use rather crude proxies to measure enforcement. Most studies rely on the scores compiled by La Porta et al. (1998). However, the scores from La Porta et al. (1998) do not specifically capture the features of regulatory accounting enforcement mechanisms but are very general proxies for the overall legal system limiting more specific conclusions on the quality of accounting enforcement bodies. Studies solely relying on a country's legal origin (code law versus common law) for measuring enforcement quality are even more problematic since the measure most likely covers a wide range of institutional factors and not only the enforcement quality of a country (similar Burgstahler et al. 2006).

Moreover, the scores compiled by La Porta et al. (1998) are now quite outdated failing to capture the current status of an enforcement system in a country. This is especially relevant since many countries have improved their enforcement structures in the last decade as reaction to accounting scandals (and legal requirements for example from the EU) and set up accounting enforcement bodies.

4.2. Impact on Disclosure Quality

Due to principal agent conflicts and contractual agreements managers have an incentive to conceal the company's true performance for their own benefits (Shleifer and Vishny 1997). Effective enforcement systems monitoring and disciplining the manager for misreporting can reduce these agency problems. Due to the deterrent effect resulting from enforcement systems enforcement is assumed to have an impact on managers' disclosure behavior. However, enforcement systems differ across countries (see section 2) and might not be equally effective. Accordingly, managers' disclosure behavior is expected to depend on the effectiveness of the enforcement system in place.

There are several studies investigating the relationship between enforcement and managers' disclosure behavior. To measure the level of compliance with mandatory disclosure requirements Glaum and Street (2003) use a self-constructed checklist while Hope (2003) relies on the disclosure list provided by the Center for International Financial Analysis and Research (CIFAR). Based on these checklists disclosure indices are calculated with a high score indicating a high compliance level. Aerts and Tarca (2010) assessing the attributes of managers' performance explanations in management commentary reports apply a list of self constructed attributes (see table 6).

The studies analyzing the relationship between enforcement mechanisms and disclosure behavior can be divided in cross country and single country studies. For measuring the strength of enforcement Hope (2003) uses five country-level variables in his cross country study: (1) "audit spending" – measured as percentage of total audit fees of the top ten audit firms in a country on gross domestic product; (2) "existence of insider trading laws" – coded as a binary variable; (3) "efficiency of the judicial system" – score provided by La Porta et al. (1998) measuring the efficiency and integrity of the legal environment of a country; (4) "rule of law" – score compiled by La Porta et al. (1998) measuring the law and order tradition of a country; and (5) "shareholder rights" – score provided by La Porta et al. (1998) measuring the protection of shareholders (for further details see La Porta et al. 1998). To aggregate the scores Hope (2003) applies factor analysis. For their cross country study Aerts and Tarca (2010) use the mean score of two measures provided by La Porta et al. (2006): (1) "public enforcement" – capturing the characteristics of the supervisory body, its rule-making and investigative power, applicable sanctions and stop and do orders; and (2) "litigation standard" – measuring procedural difficulties in recovering losses from the issuer, the distributors and the accountants in a civil liability case (see table 7).

The studies analyzing the disclosure behavior of managers provide evidence that there is a positive link between enforcement and disclosure behavior (see table 8). Hope (2003) finds that strong enforcement is positively related to higher disclosure scores and higher analyst forecast accuracy indicating that enforcement provides incentives to managers to comply with disclosure requirements, which in turn, reduce analysts' uncertainties about a firm's future performance. Analyzing the explanations of financial performance in management commentary reports Aerts and Tarca (2010) find significant differences between the USA, Canada, U.K. and Australia with respect to the extent as well as the specific characteristics of the provided explanations. Institutional factors and related differences in enforcement regimes are considered to impact the content of management commentary reports.

Finally, Glaum and Street (2003) investigate for the German New Market firms' compliance with IFRS or US-GAAP disclosure requirements respectively. Their results reveal considerable non-compliance with relevant disclosure rules especially for companies that are not cross listed in the US highlighting the impact of the SEC enforcement on disclosure compliance.

Table 7. Proxies for measuring the strength of enforcement in cross country studies assessing disclosure quality

		Model	Measurement
Study	Hope (2003)	• Mueller et al. (1994) • Bhattacharya & Daouk (2002) • La Porta et al. (1998)	Mean score across: • audit spending • insider trading laws • legal system efficiency • rule of law • shareholder protection
	Aerts & Tarca (2010)	La Porta et al. (2006)	Mean score across: • litigation standard • public enforcement index

Table 8. Impact of enforcement on disclosure behavior

		Measurement	Years analyzed	Countries analyzed	Findings: Impact of enforcement on disclosure behavior
Cross country study	Hope (2003)	Score	1991 to 1993	Austria, Belgium, Denmark, Finland, France, Germany, Italy, Japan, Netherlands, Norway, Portugal, Spain, Sweden, Sitzerland, Australia, Canada, Hong Kong, Ireland, New Zealand, South Africa, U.K., USA	+
	Aerts & Tarca (2010)	Score	2003	Australia, Canada, U.K., USA	+
Single country study	Glaum & Street (2003)	-	2000	Germany	significant differences between companies that are due to a cross listing subject to SEC enforcement and companies that are not subject to SEC enforcement

Key:
+ means that enforcement positively influences the disclosure behavior

In summary, the empirical literature on management's disclosure behavior provides evidence on the impact of enforcement on the financial reporting behavior of managers. Research reveals not all enforcement systems to be equally effective (see especially Hope 2003 and Glaum and Street 2003). The empirical findings are subject to several caveats confining the conclusions that can be derived for accounting enforcement systems. First, major limitations result from the difficulties associated with measuring the strength of a country's enforcement system. Both cross-country studies included in this review capture with their measure various institutional factors limiting more specific conclusions on the quality of a country's accounting enforcement system (for details see our arguments in section 4.1). Second, the application of self-constructed checklists to assess the disclosure behavior of managers makes it difficult to replicate the findings if judgment is necessary to construct the metric (Healy and Palepu 2001). Third, responding to accounting scandals many countries have reformed their accounting enforcement during the last few years. Therefore, the findings provided in older studies may be outdated for various jurisdictions.

CONCLUSION

The literature discussed in this chapter supports the following general conclusions: (1) Enforcement bodies vary across countries not only with respect to their structure but also with respect to their audit procedures and competencies. (2) Managers from companies subject to enforcement actions experience a higher management-turnover and reductions in performance based compensations. (3) Strong enforcement is associated with lower earnings management and higher disclosure quality indicating that enforcement can mitigate principal agent conflicts by the deterrent effect it provides.

Despite the progress in enforcement studies in the last 15 years, there are some implications for future research: (1) Studies investigating the consequences companies take after enforcement actions to sanction their management's reporting behavior provide only partially insight into companies' sanction mechanisms. Since causal effects for individual managers have not been analyzed yet, a comprehensive picture on the sanctions an individual manager experiences from its firm after found accountable for misreporting is still missing. The question remains which sanctions are applied to which manager and for which reporting infringements? In addition, so far firms' sanctions for managers following enforcement actions have only been assessed for some countries (US and China) leaving the question to which extent the research findings from these countries equally apply to other jurisdictions. (2) Cross country research assessing the relationship between enforcement quality and earnings management/managers' disclosure behavior generally applies rather crude proxies for measuring the strength of an enforcement system thereby capturing a great variety of institutional factors. Accordingly, very little is known about the effectiveness of specific enforcement bodies and about the structures and features necessary for enforcement bodies to ensure adequate enforcement. What type of enforcement (e.g. public/private body, audit frequency, sanctions) provides appropriate deterrence effects for managers and ensures effective enforcement? Is there a superior enforcement type or are different types equally effective? Answers to these questions are especially relevant for countries being in the process of establishing an enforcement body or having decided to reform their existing enforcement system. Furthermore, many cross country studies on earnings management apply the enforcement scores from La Porta et al. (1998). Since however many countries have improved their enforcement systems in the last decade responding to accounting scandals the findings provided in these studies may no longer apply and therefore call for more updated research.

REFERENCES

Aerts, W., Tarca, A. (2010). Financial performance explanations and institutional setting. *Accounting and Business Research*, 40(5), 421-450.

Agrawal, A., Cooper, T. (2009). Corporate governance consequences of accounting scandals: Evidence from top management, CFO and auditor turnover. *Working Paper*, available via: http://papers.ssrn.com/sol3/papers.cfm?abstract_id=970355 (07/11/2012).

Agrawal, A., Jaffe, J. F., Karpoff, J. M. (1999). Management turnover and governance changes following the revelation of fraud. *Journal of Law and Economics*, 42(1), 309-342.

Anderson, K. L., Yohn, T. L. (2002). The effect of 10-K restatements on firm value, information asymmetries and investor`s reliance on earnings. *Working Paper*, available via: http://papers.ssrn.com/sol3/papers.cfm?abstract_id=332380 (07/11/2012).

Armstrong, C. S., Jagolinzer, A. D., Larcker, D. F. (2010). Chief Executive Officer equity incentives and accounting irregularities. *Journal of Accounting Research*, 48(2), 225-271.

Arthaud-Day, M. L., Certo, S. T., Dalton, C. M., Dalton, D. R. (2006). A changing of the guard: Executive and director turnover following corporate financial restatements. *Academy of Management Journal*, 49(6), 1119-1136.

Ashbaugh-Skaife, H., Collins, D. W., Kinney Jr., W. R., LaFond, R. (2008). The effect of SOX internal control deficiencies and their remediation on accrual quality. *The Accounting Review*, 83(1), 217-250.

Ball, R., Kothari, S. P., Robin, A. (2000). The effect of international institutional factors on properties of accounting earnings. *Journal of Accounting and Economics*, 29(1), 1-51.

Basu, S. (1997). The conservatism principle and the asymmetric timeliness of earnings. *Journal of Accounting and Economics*, 24(1), 3-37.

Beny, L. N. (2005). Do insider trading laws matter? Some preliminary comparative evidence. *American Law and Economics Review*, 7(1), 144-183.

Bhattacharya, U., Daouk, H. (2002). The world pricing of insider trading. *Journal of Finance,* 57(1), 75-108.

Böcking, H.-J., Gros, M., Wallek, C., Worret, D. (2012). Earnings management and enforcement of accounting standards – Evidence from Germany. *Working Paper*, available via: http://papers.ssrn.com/sol3/papers.cfm?abstract_id=1755122 (07/11/2012).

Bologna, J. *Corporate fraud – The basics of prevention and detection*. Boston, 1984.

Brown, P., Tarca, A. (2005). A commentary on issues relating to the enforcement of International Reporting Standards in the EU. *European Accounting Review*, 14(1), 181-212.

Burgstahler, D. C., Dichev, I. D. (1997). Earnings management to avoid earnings decreases and losses. *Journal of Accounting and Economics*. 24(1), 99-129.

Burgstahler, D. C., Hail, L., Leuz, C. (2006). The importance of reporting incentives: Earnings management in European private and public firms. *The Accounting Review*, 81(5), 983-1016.

Burns, N., Kedia, S. (2006). The impact of performance-based compensation on misreporting. *Journal of Financial Economics*, 79(1), 35-67.

Cai, L., Rahman, A., Courtenay, S. (2008). The effect of IFRS and its enforcement on earnings management: An international comparison. *Working Paper*, available via: http://papers.ssrn.com/sol3/papers.cfm?abstract_id=1473571 (07/11/2012).

Callao, S., Jarne, J. I. (2010). Have IFRS affected earnings management in the European Union. *Accounting in Europe,* 7(2), 159-189.

Chen, G., Firth, M., Gao, N., Rui, O. (2005). Is China`s securities regulatory agency a toothless tiger? Evidence from enforcement actions. *Journal of Accounting and Public Policy*, 24(6), 451-488.

Cheng, Q., Farber, D. B. (2008). Earnings restatements, changes in CEO compensation and firm performance. *The Accounting Review*, 83(5), 1217-1249.

Christensen, H. B., Hail, L., Leuz, C. (2011). Capital-market effects of securities regulation: Hysteresis, implementation and enforcement. *Working Paper*, available via: http://www.nber.org/papers/w16737 (07/11/2012).

Collins, D., Masli, A., Reitenga, A. L., Sanchez, J. M. (2009). Earnings restatements, the Sarbanes-Oxley Act and the disciplining of Chief Financial Officers. *Journal of Accounting, Auditing and Finance,* 24(1), 1-34.

Collins, D., Reitenga, A. L., Sanchez-Cuevas, J. M. (2005). The managerial consequences of earnings restatements. *Working Paper*, available via: https://aaahq.org/MAS/mas2006/display.cfm?Filename=Manuscript66.pdf &MIMEType=application%2Fpdf (07/11/2012).

Committee of European Securities Regulators (2003). Standard No. 1 on financial information – Enforcement of standards on financial information in Europe. Available via: http://www.esma.europa.eu/system/files/ 03_073.pdf (07/11/2012).

David, R., Brierley, J. *Major legal systems in the world today*. Stevens and Sons, London, 1985.

Dechow, P. M., Dichev, I. D. (2002). The quality of accruals and earnings: The role of accrual estimation errors. *The Accounting Review*, 77(Supplement), 35-59.

Dechow, P. M., Skinner, D. (2000). Earnings management: Reconciling the views of accounting academics, practitioners and regulators. *Accounting Horizons,* 14(2), 235-250.

Dechow, P. M., Sloan, R., Sweeney, A. (1995). Detecting earnings management. *The Accounting Review*, 70(2), 193-225.

DeFond, M. L., Park, C. (2001). The reversal of abnormal accruals and the market valuation of earnings surprises. *The Accounting Review*, 76(3), 375-404.

Desai, H., Hogan, C. E., Wilkins, M. S. (2006). The reputational penalty for aggressive accounting: Earnings restatements and management turnover. *The Accounting Review*, 81(1), 83-112.

Efendi, J., Srivastava, A., Swanson, E. (2007). Why do corporate managers misstate financial statements? The role of option compensation and other factors. *Journal of Financial Economics*, 85(3), 667-708.

Ernst and Young (2010). Driving ethical growth – New markets, new challenges, 11th Global Fraud Study. Available via: http://www.ey.com/ Publication/vwLUAssets/EY-11th_Global_Fraud_Survey/$FILE/EY_11th _GLOBAL_FRAUD_Survey.pdf (07/11/2012).

Ernstberger, J., Stich, M., Vogler, O. (2012). Economic consequences of accounting enforcement reforms: The case of Germany. *European Accounting Review*, 21(2), 217-251.

Ewert, R., Wagenhofer, A. (2005). Economic effects of tightening accounting standards to restrict earnings management. *The Accounting Review*, 80(4), 1101-1124.

Fédération des Experts Comptables Européens. *Enforcement mechanisms in Europe: A preliminary investigation of oversight systems*. Available via: http://www.fee.be/publications/default.asp?library_ref=4andcontent_ref=108 (07/11/2012).

Francis, J. R. (2004). What do we know about audit quality? *The British Accounting Review,* 36(4), 345-368.

Gjesdal, F. (1981). Accounting for Stewardship. *Journal of Accounting Research,* 19(1), 208-231.

Glaum, M., Street, D. L. (2003). Compliance with the disclosure requirements of Germany`s New Market: IAS versus US-GAAP. *Journal of International Financial Management and Accounting*, 14(1), 64-100.

Hail, L., Leuz, C. (2006). International differences in the cost of equity capital: Do legal institutions and securities regulation matter? *Journal of Accounting Research*, 44(3), 485-531.

Healy, P. M. (1985). The effect of bonus schemes on accounting decisions. *Journal of Accounting and Economics*, 7(1-3), 85-107.

Healy, P. M., Palepu, K. G. (2001). Information asymmetry, corporate disclosure and the capital markets: A review of the empirical disclosure literature. *Journal of Accounting and Economics*, 31(1-3), 405-440.

Healy, P. M., Wahlen, J. M. (1999). A review of the earnings management literature and its implications for standard setting. *Accounting Horizons*, 13(4), 365-383.

Hennes, K. M., Leone, A. J., Miller, B. P. (2008). The importance of distinguishing errors from irregularities in restatement research: The case of restatements and CEO/CFO turnover. *The Accounting Review*, 83(6), 1487-1519.

Hope, O.-K. (2003). Disclosure practices, enforcement of accounting standards and analysts` forecast accuracy: An international study. *Journal of Accounting Research*, 41(2), 235-272.

Hribar, P., Jenkins, N. T. (2004). The effect of accounting restatements on earnings revisions and the estimated cost of capital. *Review of Accounting Studies*, 9(2-3), 337-356.

Karpoff, J. M., Lee, D. S., Martin, G. S. (2008a). The consequences to managers for financial misrepresentation. *Journal of Financial Economics*, 88(2), 193-215.

Karpoff, J. M., Lee, D. S., Martin, G. S. (2008b). The cost to firms of cooking the books. *Journal of Financial and Quantitative Analysis*, 43(3), 581-612.

Karpoff, J. M., Lott, J. R. (1993). The reputational penalty firms bear from committing criminal fraud. *Journal of Law and Economics*, 36(2), 757-802.

Kim, J.-B., Shi, H. (2007). International Financial Reporting Standards, institutional infrastructures and costs of equity capital around the world. *Working Paper*, available via: http://papers.ssrn.com/sol3/papers.cfm?abstract_id=984127 (07/11/2012).

Lang, M., Raedy, J. S., Wilson, W. (2006). Earnings management and cross listing: Are reconciled earnings comparable to US earnings. *Journal of Accounting and Economics*, 42(1-2), 255-283.

La Porta, R., Lopez-de-Silanes, F., Shleifer, A. (1997). Legal determinants of external finance. *Journal of Finance*, 52(3), 1113-1150.

La Porta, R., Lopez-de-Silanes, F., Shleifer, A., Vishny, R. W. (1998). Law and finance. *Journal of Political Economy*, 106(6), 1113-1155.

La Porta, R., Lopez-de-Silanes, F., Shleifer, A. (2006). What works in securities laws? *Journal of Finance*, 61(1), 1-32.

Larcker, D., Richardson, S. (2004). Fees paid to audit firms, accrual choices and corporate governance. *Journal of Accounting Research,* 42(3), 625-658.

Leng, F., Feroz, E. H., Cao, Z., Davalos, S. V. (2011). The long-term performance and failure risk of firms cited in the US SEC`s accounting and auditing enforcement releases. *Journal of Business Finance and Accounting*, 38(7), 813-841.

Leone, A. J., Liu, M. (2010). Accounting irregularities and executive turnover in founder-managed firms. *The Accounting Review*, 85(1), 287-314.

Leuz, C., Nanda, D., Wysocki, P. D. (2003). Earnings management and investor protection: An international comparison. *Journal of Financial Economics*, 69(3), 505-527.

Li, S. (2010). Does mandatory adoption of International Financial Reporting Standards in the European Union reduce the cost of equity capital? *The Accounting Review*, 85(2), 607-636.

Mueller, G. G., Gernon, H., Meek, G. *Accounting: An international perspective*. Business One Irwin, New York, 1994.

Muradoglu, G., Huskey, J. C. (2008). The impact of SEC litigation on firm value. *Working Paper*, available via: http://papers.ssrn.com/sol3/papers.cfm?abstract_id=1094948 (07/11/2012).

Nobes, C., Parker, R. B. *Comparative international accounting*. Pearson Education, London, 2008.

Nourayi, M. M. (1994). Stock price responses to the SEC`s enforcement actions. *Journal of Accounting and Public Policy*, 13(4), 333-347.

Persons, O. S. (2006). The effects of fraud and lawsuit revelation on U.S. executive turnover and compensation. *Journal of Business Ethics*, 64(4), 405-419.

Riahi-Belkaoui, A. *Accounting Theory*. Seng Lee Press, Singapore, 2004.

Securities and Exchange Commission (2010): Release Nos. 33-9109, 34-61578. Available via: http://www.sec.gov/rules/other/2010/33-9109.pdf (07/11/2012).

Shleifer, A., Vishny, R. (1997). A survey of corporate governance. *Journal of Finance*, 52(2), 737-783.

Siegel, J. (2005). Can foreign firms bond themselves effectively by renting U.S. securities laws? *Journal of Financial Economics*, 75(2), 319-359.

Skinner, D., Myers, L. (1999). Earnings momentum and earnings management. *Journal of Accounting, Auditing and Finance*, 22(2), 249-284.

Srinivasan, S. (2005). Consequences of financial reporting failure for outside directors: Evidence from accounting restatements and audit committee members. *Journal of Accounting Research*, 43(2), 291-334.

Sun, P., Zhang, Y. (2006). Is there penalty for crime: Corporate scandals and management turnover in China. *Working Paper*, available via: http://papers.ssrn.com/sol3/papers. cfm?abstract_id=891096 (07/11/2012).

Wagenhofer, A., Ewert, R. *Externe Unternehmensrechnung*. Springer Verlag, Berlin, 2003.

Wang, Y.-F., Chou, L.-T. L. (2011). Impact of restatement characteristics and subsequent earnings management on post-SOX executive turnover. *Review of Business,* 31(2), 24-50.

Wang, H., Davidson III, W. N., Wang, X. (2010). The Sarbanes-Oxley Act and CEO tenure, turnover, and risk aversion. *The Quarterly Review of Economics and Finance,* 50(3), 367-376.

Wang, J. W., Wu, W. W. (2009). The information content of stock prices, reporting incentives and accounting standards: International evidence. *Working Paper*, available via: http://www.researchgate.net/publication/

228258469_The_Information_Content_of_Stock_Prices_Reporting_Incentives_and_Accounting_Standards_International_Evidence (07/11/2012).

Wu, M. (2002). Earnings restatements: A capital market perspective. *Working Paper*, available via: http://papers.ssrn.com/sol3/papers.cfm?abstract_id=1844265 (07/11/2012).

In: Behavioral Accounting
Editor: Andreas Hellmann

ISBN: 978-1-62618-039-0
© 2013 Nova Science Publishers, Inc.

Chapter 4

A ROAD TOWARDS ENHANCED CORPORATE GOVERNANCE: (RE)CONCEPTUALIZING THE ACCOUNTING PROFESSION THROUGH AN INTEGRATED EDUCATIONAL FRAMEWORK

Nicholas McGuigan* and Thomas Kern
Department of Accounting and Corporate Governance
Macquarie University, Sydney, Australia

ABSTRACT

The market in which accounting professionals currently operate is becoming increasingly complex. Global demands, increased technology and a rapidly evolving business environment with new forms of value creation have caused increased pressure on accounting professionals to provide a broader service encompassing an progressively diverse range of stakeholders. Such a changing, complex and integrated environment demands a holistic conceptualization of the accounting profession. In order to develop an integrated perspective, accounting higher education programs need to be designed in a way that focuses on the developmental process of a professional accountant, within adopted pedagogical frameworks. By placing an emphasis on what it means to become an

* Tel: +61 2 9850 9173, E-mail: Nicholas.mcguigan@mq.edu.au.

accounting professional and an acceptance that this is a transitional process that requires critical development and attention is more likely to result in the creation of a 'learned profession', like that of law, medicine or engineering.

Keywords: Behavioral accounting, integrated reporting, corporate responsibility, accounting education, professionalization of accountants

The professional environment in which accountants operate has, in recent years, become increasingly complex. A clear focus on the 'value added' by their professional services to organisational operations is becoming the imperative. Accountants face increasing pressure to provide a service that encompasses a broader responsibility not only toward the client organizations and their stakeholders but also toward society as a whole (International Federation of Accountants, 2003). Intensifying this perceived growth in responsibility are the pressures associated with continuous changes in information and communication technologies and in accounting standards and other regulation, not least triggered by the recent Global Financial Crisis.

A growing concern over recent decades regarding the negative impacts of economic activity on the natural and social environment is evident. Since the 1980s and 90s in particular, there has been an increasing public focus on problematic environmental, social and ethical issues; concerns regarding environmental degradation, depletion of natural resources, pollution, waste, poverty, violation of human rights, distributional injustice and inter- and intra-generational inequity have increased in prominence. Consequently, there has been a growing demand from society for greater accountability and transparency of corporate business and public entities regarding social and environmental issues (Simnett et al., 2009). The recent Global Financial Crisis and its resulting colossal impact have only served to intensify such societal demand. In attempts to address the negative effects of globalization and the resulting interdependencies in economies and supply chains, the crisis has resulted in growing policy and regulatory activity worldwide.

The manner in which business is conducted today, how businesses create value and the context in which they operate has changed yet our business reporting framework remains more or less static. The traditional business reporting mechanisms we are so familiar with have been designed for an industrial world where the key focus has been on the stewardship of financial capital. Although valuable, such reporting tends to focus on a "relatively narrow account of historical performance and of the value creation process" (IIRC, 2011, p.6). We need to question whether such frameworks are relevant for a new *technological* age? An age of exponential population growth, increasing consumption, actual and prospective resource scarcity and climate change concerns. A time where a heightened imperative is placed on full disclosure and transparency of business operations, ensuring organizations are accountable for their actions and consumption. The business information needs of today are future orientated, demanding broad and market-driven risk-based information that ensures an organization's relevance and resilience in the market. Information that falls well outside our traditional reporting frameworks.

In order to meet the increasing information demands of society and the business community alike, accounting service providers need to incorporate new ways of measuring, reporting and accounting for the scarce resources available to organizations. This is evident worldwide with the recent introduction of emission trading schemes in the European Union, Australia, New Zealand, and a minority of states in the U.S. (Flannery et al., 2012), the development of water accounting standards (Egan, 2009) and the fourth generation of sustainability reporting guidelines to be released by the Global Reporting Initiative in 2013 (GRI, 2012). These examples highlight the increasing importance being placed on qualitative, non-financial information where the accounting profession is required to devise new ways of valuing, measuring, recording, analyzing and communicating accounting information. In essence, accountants need to seek new ways of seeing and making meaning of their profession.

In order to achieve such a reconceptualization, accounting service professionals need to be able to view the organization holistically as an integrated whole. This integrated perception will assist in the break down of established silos in the way information is reported and of the traditional focus primarily on financial performance and measurement. As business value creation evolves, qualitative non-financial information becomes as important as hard quantitative financial data modeling. This reconceptualization has lead to new thought leadership around accounting practice, with the formation of the International Integrated Reporting Council (IIRC) and the emergent Integrated Reporting framework.

The IIRC (2011) describe Integrated Reporting as a "bring[ing] together [of] material information about an organization's strategy, governance, performance and prospects in a way that reflects the commercial, social and environmental context within which it operates. It provides a clear and concise representation of how an organization demonstrates stewardship and how it creates value, now and in the future. Integrated Reporting combines the most material elements of information currently reported in separate reporting strands (financial, management commentary, governance and remuneration, and sustainability) in a coherent whole and importantly, shows the connectivity between them and explains how they affect the ability of an organization to create and sustain value in the short, medium and long term" (p. 8). Such an Integrated Report is envisaged by the IIRC to become the primary report issued by the organization, replacing rather than adding to existing reporting requirements.

Integrated Reporting reflects that accountants need to think in different ways. It is no longer sufficient for accountants and accounting graduates to think in isolation, report in financial silos and to possess a technical skill-based knowledge that fails to account for an organization's use of its varied and scarce resources. The emergent Integrated Reporting framework places equal importance on six key resources and relationships that an organization utilizes, described as forms of 'capital', namely, financial, manufactured, human, intellectual, natural and social capital (IIRC, 2011). It begs the question how an accountant is likely to measure, account for and report on the social capital of an organization, which involves the business' common values and beliefs, its trustworthiness and loyalty and its license to operate within society, using traditional reporting frameworks? One thing that is abundantly transparent is that accounting service professionals need to begin to learn how to think and conceptualize in an integrated manner. Such (re)thinking around what accounting information is and what the reporting process will provide, is likely to result in a radical reconceptualization of the accounting profession.

It is evident that such a reconceptualization, an ability to view the organization holistically and integrate information into a coherent whole, is proving difficult for business and the profession alike. Paul Druckman, CEO of IIRC, recently commented on the pilot project of organizations currently trialing the use of integrated reporting, "[W]ell over a 1000 are thinking they are doing integrated reports. Very few of them are integrated reports … This had resulted in bigger "combined" sustainability and financial reports rather than smaller, better targeted ones as envisaged…. [B]usinesses need[ed] to work out first what was really important to their business strategy rather than what regulations told them to do" (as quoted in Drummond, 2012). Justin Diddams, a media analyst at Citigroup, reminds us of the perceptual shift that will need to occur in order to integrate reporting effectively, when he states "I find the annual reviews [the common term being used for an integrated report] are like integrated reporting-lite versions. I still tend to see a lot of greenwash [in them]. There are some great initiatives to get companies to report on some of their inputs, but the more subjective we make the reporting the harder it becomes to compare like for like" (as quoted in Drummond, 2012). As Einstein so eloquently stated "the significant problems we have cannot be solved at the same level of thinking we were at when we created them" (as quoted in Theosophical Society in America, 1988), indicating a reconceptualization means the creation of new frameworks of understanding and ways of thinking.

In order to develop new ways of thinking and an integrated perspective, accounting higher education programs need to be designed in a way that facilitates such learning. The International Accounting Standards Board (IASB), a private standard setting body originating from London with predominantly Anglo-Saxon composition, has been instrumental in securing the implementation of International Financial Reporting Standards (IFRS) in over a hundred countries (Wild, 2009). These globally accepted accounting standards are principle-based, requiring a 'substance over form' approach that makes extensive use of accountants' professional judgments, for example, to select specific accounting policies implemented, interpret probability risk assessments and assess materiality thresholds. Despite the principle-based professional environment in which we operate, coupled with the interpretation and judgment skills now required by accountants, accounting higher education programs have continued to operate from an educational pedagogy designed around a rules-based approach.

The majority of contemporary undergraduate financial accounting courses are devised using a traditional textbook approach, compartmentalizing the discipline into 'courses', which introduce the rules, regulations and disclosure requirements of numerous financial reporting standards. Anderson (1983) warned us of such a dilemma when he stated, "[N]ew Governmental accounting standards and regulations will be promulgated in the near future, and they will be incorporated in textbooks. As a result many books – especially those pertaining to financial accounting – have become, and will continue to be, cumbersome. … Curriculum growth cannot be sustained indefinitely" (p. 5). Learners are left with a great deal of content and one might hope a thorough *procedural* understanding of accounting standards and the resulting preparation of financial statements. However, this pedagogical approach too often encourages a disjointed understanding of our discipline, where learners fail to appreciate the nature and context of accounting itself and how it is *integrated* with the rest of an organization specifically, and with society more broadly. Similar to the silo financial reporting prevalent in many organizations, where departments tend to operate independently of each other with absent context and connections, the learner experiences a siloed conceptualization of accounting. A holistic or integrated perspective can hardly be found.

In this pedagogical environment, technical accounting content takes precedent over valuable graduate capabilities and professional skills, such as a critical analytical competence, an ability to communicate and engage with clients, and developing a capacity to reflect as professionals (Albrecht and Sack, 2000; Hancock et al., 2010; Kavanagh and Drennan, 2008; McGuigan and Kern, 2009). A question arises of how accounting educators can cope with and integrate the sheer amount of authoritative financial reporting material that the accounting profession is currently engaged with? The most obvious reaction may be a counter question: should they? Is it realistic to expect accounting graduates to be conversant in every specific rule and regulation that governs financial reporting, when often this is not the case in practice? Would this be the most efficient use of time and resources for both the higher education academy and the learner, given the exposure to rapid change in business environments and, thus, in accounting regulation? Such a pursuit seems rather fruitless indeed. If compared to the legal profession, such a mastery of legal knowledge is no longer the norm with the Stanford catalog (1976) stating, "measured against the entire legal universe, no lawyer ever knows substantive law outside a single field or subfield of specialization" (p. 11).

To combat a rising level of technical accounting content a refocus should be placed on the fundamental concepts that exist within the accounting discipline. A great deal of introductory accounting courses (and their corresponding textbook resources) tend to gloss over 'threshold concepts' (Meyer and Land, 2005) that are found within the accounting curriculum, such as, materiality, depreciation, accrual versus cash accounting and valuation, in favor of presenting a comprehensive coverage of the rules in which techniques are applied. More time developing and nurturing a deep understanding and critical analytical awareness of such fundamental, threshold concepts, would bear fruitful to the current professional environment where such concepts lie at the heart of decision-making within often ambiguous contexts (Weil and McGuigan, 2010). Specific to financial accounting, this could be achieved by placing the conceptual reporting framework at the core of undergraduate course work, acting as the point of interconnection between financial accounting units, thus, presenting the reporting process as a coherent whole rather than artificially broken up, disjointed units of analysis, or university courses. Selected IFRSs that represent material importance to an individual's conceptual appreciation and understanding of accounting could be integrated across the undergraduate program in unison with such threshold concepts. Accountants are often asked to exercise a degree of professional judgment – perhaps it is time to ask the same of those who educate future accounting professionals. In this manner, learners are more likely to gain a holistic perspective of the reporting process.

A great deal of superfluous accounting knowledge and content found within the standards could often be learnt independently. This is similar to the legal and medical professions where an individual would not be expected to have a comprehensive knowledge of all living illnesses nor each existing piece of legislation, instead these could be researched and reviewed on an as needed basis. Such detailed discussions perhaps could take place outside of the traditional classroom through independent study, provided, of course, the learner is self-directed, independent and motivated (Anderson, 1983). The focus within the accounting academy may need to be more centered on the development of such human qualities.

In order to encourage a level of integrated thinking and a holistic approach to the organization, accounting education needs to provide a broader contextual appreciation with a multi-disciplinary approach. Boatsman (1983, p. 114) reminds us that "[A]ccounting does not operate in a vacuum. Many other disciplines interface with it in important ways. To insulate accounting education from these other disciplines would likely have a debilitating result". A heightened emphasis needs to be placed on accounting's interrelations and connections within an operational business environment, not only between sub-discipline topics such as, financial reporting, auditing, management accounting, information systems and controls, but also across disciplines where accounting's relationship to finance, marketing, business law and human resources is explicitly acknowledged and explored by accounting educators. A renewed focus on such linkages and multi-disciplinary perspectives is likely to appeal to a new generation of learners that are technologically advanced and used to thinking in multi lateral ways. It is with this in mind that such individuals may bring new appreciation and understanding to critical questions and problems that plague accounting thought and practice (Pathways Commission, 2012).

The recent Pathways Commission Report (2012) issued in collaboration by the American Accounting Association (AAA) and the American Institute of Certified Public Accountant's (AICPA) have called for the development of a 'learned profession' similar to that of law, medicine and engineering, through a careful integration of accounting research, education and practice for learners, practitioners and educators. In this way, they have advocated for strong linkages between research and practice, practice and education, and education and research where such interconnecting relationships are critical to the sustainability of an internationally recognized profession. Such a recommendation is not new; in fact, the first leading article published in *Journal of Accountancy* was on the topic of educating accountants. Sterrett (1905, p. 8) argued that "[T]he time has come, however, for a broader view, and it is necessary that accountants should make a concerted movement to lift the standard of preliminary education of their profession. If accountancy is to rank among other learned professions, it must require of every applicant for admission, a standard of preliminary education equivalent to that which is required by law and medicine".

In order to develop a learned profession, there is a need to focus on the developmental process of a professional accountant, within adopted pedagogical frameworks. Such engaged thought and scholarship by accounting educators need to place a heightened emphasis on what it means to become an accounting professional, an acceptance that this is a transitional process that requires critical development and attention. A need exists within accounting to (re)conceptualize and reposition undergraduate and postgraduate learning around the notion of *becoming* a professional, an explicit acknowledgement needs to be placed on such a transition from being a learner within a university context to becoming a professional, expected to be work-ready and employable within the profession. The title suggests that such a (re)conceptualization of accounting education, focusing on the individual and their behavior, constitutes a road towards enhanced corporate governance, a road acting as a metaphor for a travelled journey. Accounting educators need to explicitly recognize that such a learning journey exists and should be nurtured, where new forms of learning and student engagement around such a journey are designed, implemented and evaluated.

In doing so, the often *intangible* skills required to become a professional accountant, such as, interpersonal and written communication skills, analytical and critical reasoning, professional judgement, risk management and corporate governance awareness, emotional intelligence and reflective capacity, flexibility and adaptability, ethical reasoning, group and cooperation skills and information technology skills, are explicitly made tangible, integrated, addressed and developed within higher education programs.

A focus is therefore placed on the development and application of professional judgment and decision-making within differing contexts, where technical accounting knowledge comprises only a part of the overall equation. Such technical content knowledge now represents the norm by employers, and graduates need to be able to clearly differentiate themselves in the market place. The current standard of education may no longer be fit-for-purpose, and accounting educators are required to seek out and develop unique attributes in graduates that place them above such an expected norm. Similar to integrated reporting, where an organization is expected to integrate its many different capitals together in a common future-focused narrative, constructed around organizational strategy and the value-creation process, accounting educators need to develop such an integrated approach to curriculum design, that is future oriented, where an emphasis is placed on the integration of such intangible skills and multi-disciplinary perspectives. In this way, future graduates are able to develop learner independence that will result in a capacity to critically reflect on their actions and experiences and in a commitment to lifelong learning and professional development.

Hellmann and Scagnelli (2011) state, "[T]he importance of behavioral aspects on all dimensions of accounting is influencing the decision making of investors and other users of financial information.... It is high time that stakeholders move away from narrow approaches such as the 'economic man' and develop new frameworks in accounting and finance, which focus on people and their behavior." Such a focus of accounting and the reporting process around people and their behavior requires a changed (re) conceptualization of the accounting profession. In order to view our world differently, in a more integrated and holistic manner where businesses are operating in a complex and dynamic environment, individuals need to be provided with an education and professional development that facilitates such a perspective. It appears inevitable that such an integrated accounting educational framework will necessitate a dramatic (re)conceptualization of the education process by current and future accounting educators to create a 'learned profession', equal to that of law, medicine or engineering.

REFERENCES

Albrecht, W.S., and Sack, R.J. (2000). *Accounting Education: Charting the course through a perilous future, Accounting Education Series*, Vol. 16. Sarasota, FL: American Accounting Association.

American Accounting Association (AAA). (2012). *The Pathways Commission on Higher Education: Charting a National Strategy for the Next Generation of Accountants.* Available online at: http://commons.aaahq.org/files/0b14318188/Pathways_Commission_Final_Report_Complete.pdf. Last Accessed 21 November 2012.

Anderson, W.T. (1983). Suggested Changes in Accounting Education to meet the Demand of the Profession. *Journal of Accounting Education*, 1(2), 5-10.

Boatsman, J.R. (1983). American Law Schools: Implications for Accounting Education. *Journal of Accounting Education*, 1(1), 93-117.

Drummond, S. (2012). Long Way to go to Integrate Reporting. Available online at http://afr.com/f/free/markets/capital/cfo/long_way_to_go_to_integrate_reporting_en5uE0LSotID7GxCHwUdYJ. Last accessed 14 November 2012.

Egan, M. (2009). Sydney Water Sector Change and Industrial Water Management: research note. *Journal of Accounting and Organizational Change*, 5(2), 277-293.

Flannery, T., Beale, R., Huston, G. (2012). *The Critical Decade: International Action on Climate Change*. Canberra, Australia: Climate Commission Secretariat.

Global Reporting Initiative (GRI). (2012). *Policy will be crucial in making sustainability reporting standard practice, says global sustainability organization.* Available online at: https://www.globalreporting.org/information/news-and-press-center/Pages/Policy-will-be-crucial-in-making-sustainability-reporting-standard-practice-says-global-sustainability-organization.aspx. Last accessed 21 November 2012.

Hancock, P., Howieson, B., Kavanagh, M., Kent, J., Tempone, I. and Segal, N. (2010). Accounting for the Future. In Evans, E., Burritt, R. and Guthrie, J. (eds.) 2010. *Accounting Education at a Crossroad in 2010*. Australia: The Institute of Chartered Accountants in Australia, 54-62.

Hellmann, A. and Scagnelli, S.D. (2011). Behavioral Accounting: Shifting Away from Techniques to People, in Nelson, W.D. (Ed.). *Advances in Business and Management Volume 3*, New York: Nova Science Publications, p.133-136.

International Federation of Accountants (IFAC). (2003). *Introduction to International Education Standards*, New York: IFAC.

International Integrated Reporting Committee (IIRC). (2011). Towards Integrated Reporting: Communicating Value in the 21st Century.

Available online at: theiirc.org/wp-content/uploads/2011/09/IR-Discussion-Paper-2011_spreads.pdf. Last accessed 16 November 2012.

Kavanagh, M.H. and Drennan, L. (2008). What skills and attributes does an accounting graduate need? Evidence from student perceptions and employer expectations. *Accounting and Finance*, 48(2), 279-300.

McGuigan, N. and Kern, T. (2009). The Reflective Accountant: Changing students' perceptions of traditional accounting through reflective educational practice. *International Journal of Learning*, 16(9), 49-68.

Meyer, J.H.F. and Land, R. (2005). Threshold concepts and troublesome knowledge (2): epistemological considerations and a conceptual framework for teaching and learning, *Higher Education*, 49, 373-388.

Simnett, R., Vanstraelen, A., Chua, W.F. (2009). Assurance on Sustainability Reports: An International Comparison. *The Accounting Review*, 84(3), 937-967.

Stanford Catalog. (1976). *The Study of Law at Stanford*. U.S.: Stanford University.

Sterrett, J.E. (1905). Education and training of a certified public accountant. *Journal of Accountancy,* 1(1), 1-15.

Theosophical Society in America. (1988). *The Quest, Volumes 1-2*. U.S.: Theosophical Society in America.

Weil, S. and McGuigan, N. (2010). Identifying threshold concepts in the bank reconciliation section of an introductory accounting course: creating an ontological shift for students, in Meyer, J.H.F., Land, R. and Ballie, C. (Eds) (2010). *Threshold Concepts and Transformational Learning*, Rotterdam, The Netherlands: Sense Publishers, 333-345.

Wild, K. (2009). *Use of IFRSs by jurisdiction*. London, Deloitte Touche Tohmatsu.

In: Behavioral Accounting
Editor: Andreas Hellmann

ISBN: 978-1-62618-039-0
© 2013 Nova Science Publishers, Inc.

Chapter 5

NEUROSCIENCES: THE NEXT FRONTIER OF BEHAVIORAL ACCOUNTING?

***Andreas Hellmann*[1,*] *and Lurion De Mello*[2,†]**
[1]Department of Accounting and Corporate Governance,
Faculty of Business and Economics,
Macquarie University, Sydney, Australia
[2]Department of Applied Finance and Actuarial Studies,
Faculty of Business and Economics,
Macquarie University, Sydney, Australia

At its core, accounting is about judgments and decisions. Principles-based standards require accountants to use their professional judgments in preparing financial statements, auditors use their professional judgments in verifying the financial statements and investors largely base their financial decisions on financial statements. As a result of this, research related to judgments and decision making in accounting is arguably the largest and most influential area of accounting research. The diversity of this research area allows researchers to adopt a range of different research methods, but we suggest that research related to judgments and decision making should best be based on experiments. Bonner (2008) argues that experiments have many advantages over other methods to examine judgments and decisions. She states that

* Tel: +61 2 9850 4055. E-mail: andreas.hellmann@mq.edu.au.
† Tel: +61 2 9850 9179, E-mail: lurion.demello@mq.edu.au.

"experiments allow the researcher to control for alternative explanations for results through random assignment of subjects to treatments; systematic manipulation of variables of interest; control of variables not of interest by, for example, holding them constant; and valid and reliable measurement of variables" (p.19). However, mainstream accounting research sometimes attempts to examine behavioral issues based on quantitative models that are built on simplistic assumptions underlying human behavior (see chapter 2 for more details). Instead of relying on mathematical models, we make a case for the adoption of neurosciences in accounting that capture the behavioral characteristics of individuals (and groups). To illustrate the advantages, we use cultural studies in accounting as an example.

An important area of research regarding judgments and decision making is international accounting. In recent years, international accounting convergence has been one of the key advances in accounting, which can be defined as the process of replacing national accounting standards with a single set of standards (Whittington 2005). The International Accounting Standards Board (IASB), a private body standard setter based in London, develops such a set of globally accepted accounting standards. Indeed, the IASB was highly successful in recent years to establish their International Financial Reporting Standards (IFRS) as globally accepted accounting standards with over 115 countries permitting or requiring them to be used for financial accounting purposes. The development of IFRS has been supported by the notion that a single set of high-quality global accounting standards is an important means of enhancing comparability of financial statements, helping investors (and other stakeholders) to make better financial decisions. In other words, the IASB assumes that financial statements are comparable across countries if accountants all over the world apply IFRS. However, this notion is too simplistic if behavioral aspects are taken into consideration.

Differences in, for example, legal systems, taxation, sources of finance, inflation, political ties, and culture cause diversity in accounting practices (Salter and Doupnik 1992, Doupnik and Salter 1995, Nobes 1998, Jaggi and Low 2000, Patel et al. 2002, Evans 2004, Richardson 2007). These contextual factors are deeply embedded in the accounting environment of a country. As such, they may not be simply changed and could act as impediments to similar adoption of IFRS across countries. In addition, achieving comparability in financial reporting depends also on a consistent interpretation and application of IFRS across countries. Social, political, economic and cultural factors in countries influence accountants' professional judgments and differences across countries. This may lead to an inconsistent interpretation and application of

IFRS. Indeed, in view of the fact that IFRS are principles-based standards, the extensive application of professional judgment is expected of professional accountants. For example, the conceptual framework of the IASB is characterized by the concept "substance over form", which highlights that the economic "substance" of a business transaction is more important than its legal "form". Several studies provided evidence that professional judgment is applied inconsistently across countries, especially if countries have accounting environments that are different from those in Anglo-American countries where IFRS were developed (Doupnik and Richter 2003, 2004). As such, it may be too simplistic to assume that the worldwide adoption of IFRS will automatically lead to comparability in financial reporting.

In this context, culture has long been considered a factor that affects judgment and decision making of professional accountants and the accounting environment of a country (Gray 1988, Perera, 1989). Gernon and Wallace (1995), for example, refer to culture in their accounting ecology framework as an important element within society that shapes the environment in which accounting operates. The importance of culture in the international accounting literature is also reflected in an increasing number of studies that provide evidence that aspects of culture influence various dependent variables such as external auditor's appointment and independence (Patel and Psaros 2000, Hope et al. 2008), professional ethics (Cohen et al. 1995), accountants' values and judgments (Doupnik and Richter 2004, Doupnik and Riccio 2006), and standard setting (Ding et al. 2005).

So how does this all tie up to the area of neuroscience? Many cross-cultural accounting studies can be criticized because they operationalize culture as a "black-box" or simply "pick and choose" suitable cultural dimensions, for example Hofstede's (1980) five-dimension scheme and related scales, in order to develop hypothesis and explain dependent variables (see for example, Patel 2004, for a review). However, such an approach is likely to show only very crude differences between individuals. It may be suitable for classifying groups of people based on limited dimensions, but it may not be very useful in explaining the behavior of individuals. Importantly, Bonner (2008, p. 105) points out that "people from different cultures differ in their knowledge, knowledge structure, and cognitive processes". She refers to Nisbett (2003), for example, who provides evidence that "people from different cultural groups categorize things differently and also differ in their need to categorize information" (Bonner 2008, p. 105). While we agree that cultural differences may influence aspects such as learning behavior and moral values, we believe that accounting researchers relying entirely on cultural dimensions to explain difference in human behavior fail on one important dimension. They ignore the core aspect of human behavior which is determined by the level of brain activity. In this context, neuroscience can be very useful. Instead of relying on observations or quantitative studies that categorize people on simplistic dimensions, researchers should explore brain activity and thought processes. This would enable researchers to analyze individuals, and not groups of people who may not be as homogenous as the quantitative results are suggesting.

Neuroscientists study actual processes of the human brain and brain activity associated with specific locations within the brain. Such research provides hard physiological evidence on judgments and decision making, and importantly, enables researchers to better understand the biological basis for the behaviors they observed in experiments. Importantly, neurosciences are not restricted to "brain scanning" alone. Tools such as eye-tracking and skin conductance have been used to examine perception and emotions. These methods can help penetrate the abovementioned "black-box" by matching observed decisions with activity in a portion of the brain or other physiological reactions. We believe that such hard physiological evidence is urgently needed to verify cultural and other studies in accounting. Capturing brain activity and physiological reaction of individuals is likely to eventually help researchers in identifying sub groups within cultures.

REFERENCES

Bonner, S. E. (2008). *Judgment and decision making in accounting*. Pearson Prentice Hall, New Jersey.

Cohen, J.R., Pant, L.W., Sharp, D.J. (1995). An exploratory examination of international differences in auditors ethical perceptions. *Behavioral Research in Accounting*, 7(1), 37-64.

Ding, Y., Jeanjean, T., Stolowy, H. (2005). Why do national GAAP differ from IAS? The role of culture. *International Journal of Accounting*, 40(4), 325-350.

Doupnik, T.S., Richter, M. (2004). The impact of culture on the interpretation of "in text" verbal probability expressions. *Journal of International Accounting Research*, 3(1), 1-20.

Doupnik, T.S., Riccio, E.L. (2006). The influence of conservatism and secrecy on the interpretation of verbal probability expressions in the Anglo and Latin cultural areas. *International Journal of Accounting*, 41(1), 237-261.

Doupnik, T.S., Salter, S.B. (1995). External environmental and accounting practice: A preliminary test of a general model of international accounting development. *International Journal of Accounting*, 30(2), 189-207.

Evans, L. (2004). Language, translation and the problem of international accounting communication. *Accounting, Auditing and Accountability Journal*, 17(2), 210-248.

Gray, S.J. (1988). Towards a theory of cultural influence on the development of accounting systems internationally. *Abacus*, 24(1), 1-15.

Gernon, H., Wallace, R.S.C. (1995). International accouting research: A review of its ecology, contending theories and methodologies. *Journal of Accounting Literature*, 14(1), 54-106.

Hope, O.-K., Kang, T., Thomas, W., Yoo, Y.K. (2008). Culture and auditor choice: A test of the secrecy hypothesis. *Journal of Accounting and Public Policy*, 27(5), 357-373.

Jaggi, B., Low, P.Y. (2000). Impact of culture, market forces, and legal system on financial disclosure. International Journal of Accounting, 35(4), 495-519.

Nisbett, R. (2003). *The geography of thought: How Asians and Westerners think differently and why*. Free Press, New York.

Nobes, C. (1998). Towards a general model of the reasons for international differences in financial reporting. *Abacus*, 34(2), 162-187.

Patel, C. (2004). Some theoretical and methodological suggestions for cross-cultural accounting studies. *International Journal of Accounting, Auditing and Performance Evaluation*, 1(1), 61-84.

Patel, C., Harrison, G.L., McKinnon, J.L. (2002). Cultural influences on judgments of professional accountants in auditor-client conflict resolution. *Journal of International Financial Management and Accounting*, 13(1), 1-31.

Patel, C., Psaros, J. (2000). Perceptions of external auditors' independence: Some cross-cultural evidence. *British Accounting Review*, 32(3), 311-338.

Perera, H. (1989). Towards a framework to analyze the impact of culture on accounting. *International Journal of Accounting*, 24(1), 42-56.

Richardson, G. (2007). The influence of culture on tax systems internationaly: A theoretical and empirical analysis. *Journal of International Accounting Research*, 6(1), 57-79.

Salter, S.B., Doupnik, T.S. (1992). *The relationship between legal systems and accounting practices: A classification exercise*. JAI Press, London.

Whittington, G. (2005). The adoption of international accounting standards in the EU. *European Accounting Review*, 14, 127-153.

INDEX

A

accountability, 86
accounting, 2, 3, 7, 8, 12, 13, 26, 31, 32, 33, 35, 36, 41, 42, 43, 44, 46, 47, 48, 51, 55, 56, 58, 59, 60, 61, 62, 63, 64, 65, 66, 68, 72, 74, 76, 78, 79, 80, 81, 82, 83, 85, 86, 87, 88, 89, 90, 91, 92, 93, 95, 97, 98, 99, 100, 101
accounting education, viii, 86, 91, 92, 93
accounting fraud, 56, 63, 68
accounting profession, viii, 12, 85, 87, 88, 90, 91, 92, 93
accounting research, vii, 3, 92, 97, 99
accounting standards, 43, 44, 56, 65, 67, 68, 73, 79, 81, 83, 86, 87, 89, 98, 101
acquisitions, 9
activity theory, 17
adaptability, 92
adaptation, 39
adjustment, 39, 40, 46, 50
advancements, 10, 47
age, 87
agencies, 15, 61, 70
altruism, 36, 52
altruistic behavior, 36, 37
anchoring, 39, 40, 46, 51, 52
annual review, 88
aspiration, 38, 39
assessment, 7, 71
assets, 4, 35, 42
asymmetry, 81
attitudes, 12, 42, 47
audit, 7, 12, 26, 44, 47, 56, 57, 59, 60, 63, 67, 75, 77, 81, 82, 83, 91
authenticity, 7
authority, 16, 60
aversion, 45
awareness, 90, 92

B

background information, 12
balance sheet, 10
bargaining, 37, 49
behavioral aspects, vii, 2, 33, 43, 47, 93, 98
behavioral sciences, 17
behaviors, 16, 100
belief systems, 52
benefits, 4, 35, 37, 44, 63, 67, 74
bias, 13, 17, 41
bounds, 41
brain, 32, 39, 100
browsing, 20, 21
business environment, 23, 85, 90, 91
business partners, 59
business strategy, 88
businesses, 86, 93
buyers, 35, 42

C

capital markets, vii, 10, 24, 26, 32, 43, 81
cash, 10, 35, 90
category b, 39
challenges, 33, 80
charities, 35, 36
China, 5, 64, 77, 79, 83
classification, 101
clients, 16, 90
climate change, 87
cognitive abilities, 38, 41
cognitive capacities, 39
cognitive function, 49
cognitive process, 99
cognitive style, 44
commercial, 8, 87
common law, 61, 70, 74
communication, 5, 6, 8, 10, 17, 18, 21, 86, 92, 101
communication technologies, 86
community, 53, 87
compensation, 58, 62, 66, 79, 80, 83
competitors, 12
compliance, 59, 60, 68, 74, 75
composition, 89
computation, 34
computer, 4, 15, 16, 20, 23, 40
computing, 34, 42
conceptualization, 85, 90, 92, 93
conductance, 100
conference, 3, 6, 8, 14, 17, 29
confirmation bias, 13, 41
conflict, 101
conflict resolution, 101
conformity, 52
conjunction fallacy, 51
connectivity, 88
consensus, 53
consent, 53
constituents, 35
consumer choice, 51
consumption, 33, 87
content analysis, 2, 27
convergence, 50, 98
cooperation, 92
corporate governance, 3, 5, 82, 83, 92
corporate social responsibility, 3, 9, 24
corruption, 70
cost, 6, 8, 10, 20, 24, 35, 36, 37, 48, 53, 81, 82
course work, 90
creditors, 59
critical thinking, 39
criticism, 52
cultural differences, 99
cultural influence, 101
culture, 43, 48, 98, 99, 100, 101
curriculum, 90, 93

D

decision makers, 10, 23, 35, 45
decision-making process, 17
deficiencies, 78
Department of Justice, 64
dependent variable, 99
depreciation, 90
detection, 79
deterrence, 57, 77
developed countries, 25
developmental process, 85, 92
directors, 12, 58, 63, 83
disclosure, 44, 55, 56, 58, 60, 73, 74, 75, 76, 77, 81, 87, 89, 101
disposition, 34
distribution, 8, 33
diversity, 97, 98
dominance, 43

E

earnings, 55, 58, 60, 63, 68, 69, 70, 71, 72, 77, 78, 79, 80, 81, 82, 83
ecology, 99, 101
economic activity, 86
economic performance, 68
economic relations, 34
economic theory, 32, 34

economics, 31, 32, 33, 34, 35, 36, 42, 46, 48, 49, 50, 52
education, 86, 89, 91, 92, 93
educators, 90, 91, 92, 93
emission, 87
emotional experience, 22
emotional intelligence, 92
empathy, 35
empirical studies, 72
employers, 93
enforcement, vii, 7, 53, 55, 56, 57, 58, 59, 60, 61, 62, 63, 64, 65, 66, 67, 68, 69, 70, 71, 72, 74, 75, 76, 77, 79, 80, 81, 82, 83
enforcement actions, vii, 55, 57, 58, 59, 60, 61, 62, 64, 65, 66, 68, 72, 73, 77, 79, 83
engineering, 86, 92, 93
environment, 2, 16, 17, 19, 53, 55, 61, 70, 75, 85, 86, 89, 90, 93, 98, 99
environmental degradation, 86
environmental issues, 86
environmental variables, 19
environments, 16, 99
equities, 10
equity, 9, 10, 11, 48, 53, 66, 78, 81, 82
equity market, 48
ethical issues, 86
ethics, 35, 99
Europe, 4, 11, 27, 28, 50, 60, 79, 80, 81
European Union (EU), 74, 79, 82, 87, 101
evidence, 4, 8, 10, 12, 13, 26, 33, 37, 38, 39, 40, 41, 42, 43, 44, 45, 46, 48, 56, 58, 63, 64, 66, 68, 71, 75, 76, 79, 83, 99, 100, 101
evolution, 51
exercise, 91, 101
expenditures, 68
experimental design, 37, 50
experimental economics, 35, 48
expertise, 27, 56, 60
exposure, 20, 90
extraction, 6
eye-tracking, 100

F

factor analysis, 75
financial capital, 86
financial crisis, 32
financial data, 7, 10, 59, 87
financial information, vii, 3, 4, 6, 7, 8, 9, 12, 23, 24, 26, 33, 44, 45, 47, 59, 60, 80, 87, 93
financial markets, 11, 31, 35, 42, 43, 44, 59
financial performance, 75, 87
financial reports, 7, 55, 56, 57, 58, 68, 88
firm size, 8
firm value, 78, 83
flexibility, 92
fMRI, 49
force, 63
forecasting, 29
foreign firms, 83
formation, 87
framing, 45, 49, 51
France, 4, 61
fraud, 56, 63, 78, 79, 82, 83
free riders, 36
funds, 11

G

gambling, 40
genre, 17
geography, 101
Germany, 1, 4, 11, 26, 50, 55, 61, 71, 79, 81
glasses, 40
globalization, 86
goods and services, 33
governance, 59, 60, 61, 63, 65, 66, 78, 87
governments, 44
gross domestic product, 75
grounding, 34
growth, 80, 86, 89
guidance, 2, 7, 29

guidelines, 87

H

hair, 40
health, 17
higher education, 85, 89, 90, 92
history, 48
homo economicus model, vii, 35, 36, 37, 38, 39, 43, 46, 47, 52
Hong Kong, 7
human, vii, 2, 3, 11, 13, 14, 15, 16, 17, 18, 23, 24, 31, 34, 39, 41, 45, 46, 48, 52, 86, 88, 91, 98, 100
human behavior, vii, 18, 24, 34, 45, 46, 98, 100
human brain, 48, 100
human resources, 91
human right, 86
human rights, 86
hypertext, 21
hypothesis, 3, 41, 71, 99, 101
hypothesis formulation, 3

I

ideal, 32, 41
illusion, 13
image, vii, 31, 46, 49
improvements, 14
impulses, 42
income, 6, 10
independence, 93, 99, 101
indexing, 12
individuals, 2, 4, 10, 34, 35, 36, 42, 44, 47, 91, 93, 98, 99, 100
inequity, 86
infancy, 34
inferences, 65
inflation, 98
information processing, 23, 27, 48
information retrieval, 14, 26
information seeking, 2, 3, 4, 11, 14, 15, 16, 17, 18, 19, 20, 21, 22, 24, 25, 26, 29
information technology, 92
insider trading, 70, 75, 79
institutional infrastructure, 82
institutions, 58, 59, 61, 81
integration, 92, 93
integrity, 70, 75
intellect, 52
intermediaries, 3, 13
internet financial reporting, vii, 2, 4, 6, 7, 8, 10, 24, 25, 26
interrelations, 91
investment, 2, 10, 11, 12, 13, 35, 38, 40
investors, vii, 1, 2, 3, 5, 6, 7, 10, 11, 12, 13, 24, 27, 28, 32, 33, 35, 40, 42, 43, 47, 51, 56, 70, 93, 97, 98
IRC, 88
isolation, 88

J

jurisdiction, 95

L

labor market, 58, 66, 67, 68
labor relations, 9, 24
law enforcement, 61
laws, 70, 75, 79, 82, 83
lead, 22, 40, 59, 65, 87, 98
leadership, 87
learners, 89, 91, 92
learning, 89, 92, 95, 99
learning behavior, 99
legislation, 91
lifelong learning, 93
linguistics, 16
litigation, 61, 62, 75, 83
loyalty, 88

M

macro-economic models, 32, 34
macroeconomics, 34
mainstream accounting research, vii, 98

management, vii, 12, 16, 17, 35, 51, 55, 56, 57, 58, 59, 60, 61, 63, 65, 66, 68, 69, 70, 71, 72, 74, 75, 76, 77, 78, 79, 80, 81, 82, 83, 88, 91
manipulation, 98
marketing, 45, 91
MAS, 80
mass, 35, 42
mathematics, 34
measurement(s), 44, 69, 70, 87, 98
media, 17, 88
medical, 91
medicine, 86, 92, 93
memory, 39, 40, 48
memory capacity, 39
mental image, 40
mental state, 24
metaphor, 32, 92
methodology, 3
microeconomics, 34
models, 14, 16, 29, 32, 34, 35, 42, 70, 98
momentum, 83
motivation, 34, 36, 37, 44
multimedia, 24
music, 10, 45

N

national economies, 34
National Strategy, 94
natural resources, 86
natural science, 17, 34
negative effects, 67, 86
negotiation, 41
Netherlands, 95
network theory, 17
neurobiology, 17
neuroscience, 99
neutral, vii, 31, 33, 42, 43, 44, 47
New York Stock Exchange, 5, 7, 28
New Zealand, 7, 87

O

OECD, 30
online information, 1, 11
operations, 9, 86, 87
optimization, 39
oversight, 56, 57, 60, 81
ownership, 10, 27, 70

P

participants, vii, 12, 21, 31, 32, 35, 41, 42, 43, 44, 46, 47
pedagogy, 89
penalties, 58, 66, 67, 68
permission, iv
Philadelphia, 26
Philippines, 71
physical environment, 19
policy, 26, 29, 44, 86
policy options, 44
political power, 53
politics, 16
pollution, 86
population, 87
population growth, 87
portability, 12
portfolio, 13, 50
poverty, 16, 86
precedent, 90
preparation, iv, 44, 46, 47, 89
prevention, 79
principles, 14, 44, 45, 99
private investors, vii, 1, 2, 3, 6, 10, 11, 12, 13, 14, 24
probability, 39, 40, 44, 48, 50, 51, 68, 89, 100
probability judgment, 51
problem-solving, 18
professional development, 93
professionalization, 86
professionals, 12, 85, 87, 88, 90, 91
profitability, 8
project, 88
protection, 70, 75, 82
psychology, 17, 26, 32, 33, 34, 35, 36, 45, 46, 48, 49, 50, 51
public corporations, 2

public interest, 53
publishing, 61
punishment, 37, 52

Q

qualitative research, 2
query, 16

R

random assignment, 98
rationality, 34, 36, 38, 39, 41, 46, 49, 50, 51
reactions, 100
real time, 3, 4
reasoning, 39, 46, 51, 63, 92
recall, 14, 40
reciprocity, 38, 48, 49, 52
recognition, 44, 56
recommendations, iv, 20
reconciliation, 95
reforms, 71, 78, 81
regulations, 7, 88, 89
relevance, 17, 20, 21, 23, 47, 49, 87
reliability, 41, 56
religious beliefs, 37
remediation, 78
representativeness, 39, 46
representativeness heuristic, 39, 46
reputation, 59, 67
requirements, 15, 17, 57, 74, 75, 81, 88, 89
researchers, 3, 4, 15, 17, 21, 25, 26, 33, 47, 70, 97, 99, 100
reserves, 9
resilience, 87
resource allocation, 59
resources, 88, 90
response, 39
retaliation, 49
revenue, 44
rhetoric, 45
rights, iv, 53, 70, 75
risk, vii, 2, 13, 19, 32, 44, 45, 46, 62, 70, 82, 83, 87, 89, 92
risk assessment, 89
risk aversion, 83
risk management, 92
risks, 13, 31, 46
roots, 14
Royal Society, 14
rule of law, 70, 75
rules, 60, 68, 75, 83, 89, 90

S

sanctions, 53, 55, 57, 58, 59, 60, 61, 62, 65, 67, 71, 75, 77
SAP, 5
Sarbanes-Oxley Act, 63, 80, 83
scarce resources, 34, 87, 88
scholarship, 92
science, 3, 14, 15, 16, 28, 33, 40
scope, 35, 58, 60, 66, 68
securities, 79, 80, 81, 82, 83
security, 6
self-confidence, 22
self-efficacy, 19
self-interest, 34, 35, 36, 38, 52
sellers, 35, 42
senses, 15
service provider, 87
shareholders, 10, 12, 27, 35, 75
Singapore, 83
smoking, 41
social behavior, 48
social capital, 16, 88
social environment, 53, 86
social learning, 19
social learning theory, 19
social network, 17
social norms, 37, 52
social responsibility, 3, 9, 24
social sciences, 26
social services, 16
social status, 53
social workers, 16
society, 47, 86, 87, 88, 90, 99

sociology, 16, 51
software, 21
solution, 39, 42, 58, 59
specialists, 21
specialization, 90
specific knowledge, 63
stakeholders, vii, 3, 6, 33, 44, 45, 47, 59, 68, 85, 86, 93, 98
state, 16, 40, 50, 93, 97
statistics, 9, 34
stock, 5, 7, 8, 9, 60, 63, 67, 70, 83
stock exchange, 7, 8, 60
stock markets, 70
stock price, 5, 9, 63, 83
structure, 60, 68, 77, 99
structuring, 68
substitutes, 5
supply chain, 86
surplus, 37
sustainability, 53, 87, 88, 92, 94
synthesis, 47

T

tactics, 22
tax system, 101
taxation, 98
techniques, 14, 45, 90
technological advancement, 34
technology, 1, 10, 14, 15, 27, 28, 85
textbook, 89, 90
theoretical development, 3, 17
thoughts, 22
trade, 13, 51
training, 95
traits, 40
transactions, 56, 68
transcripts, 6
translation, 101
transparency, 27, 86, 87
treatment, 24
trustworthiness, 88
turnover, 58, 63, 64, 65, 66, 77, 78, 80, 81, 82, 83

U

United Kingdom (UK), 4, 7, 26
United Nations, 41
United States (US), 4, 5, 7, 45, 61, 75
updating, 12, 50

V

valuation, 28, 80, 90
variables, vii, 18, 19, 24, 38, 52, 70, 75, 98
variety of domains, 41
virtual communities, 17
vision, 12

W

waste, 86
water, 87
wealth, 11, 66
web, 3, 4, 5, 6, 7, 8, 9, 10, 11, 12, 13, 16, 20, 21, 22, 23, 24, 25, 26, 27, 29, 45
web sites, 3, 4, 5, 6, 7, 8, 9, 10, 11, 12, 13, 21, 23, 24, 26, 27, 29, 45
websites, 13, 21
work environment, 19
World Wide Web, 4, 20
worldwide, 86, 87, 99

X

XML, 26